W9-CLZ-001

The Ethics of Necropolis

The Ethics of Necropolis

*An Essay on
the Military-Industrial Complex
and the Quest
for a Just Peace*

Max L. Stackhouse

Beacon Press   Boston

CARNEGIE LIBRARY
LIVINGSTONE COLLEGE
SALISBURY, N. C. 28144

Copyright © 1971 by Max L. Stackhouse

Library of Congress catalog card number: 77–136234

International Standard Book Number: 0–8070–1144–4

Beacon Press books are published under the auspices
of the Unitarian Universalist Association

Published simultaneously in Canada by Saunders of Toronto, Ltd.

All rights reserved

Printed in the United States of America

301.59
St775

To my children,
Dale, David, and Sara
May they live in a world
governed by a Just Peace

80555

Contents

Acknowledgments

The following study was written under grants from the National and Women's Divisions of the General Board of Missions and the General Board of Christian Social Concerns of the United Methodist Church in cooperation with the Office of Church and Society, Board of Christian Education of the United Presbyterian Church in the U.S.A., with extensive assistance from the Boston Industrial Mission and Andover Newton Theological School. I deeply appreciate the help of Shirley Greene, Benjamin Sissel, Luther Tyson, Peggy Billings, Norman Faramelli, and their colleagues from these institutions for their support, encouragement, interest, and criticism. Neither these bodies nor the executives mentioned is responsible for the contents, views, or inadequacies of this document. But from my perspective, the engagement of denominational bodies and agencies in this sort of research is beneficial to both academic life and the life of the churches. Theory without supporting institutions is ineffective; institutions without theory are vacuous. It is my hope that the cooperation experienced in the course of this study will facilitate a closer link of moral reflection and moral organization.

Finally, I want to thank Paul Deats, Ralph Potter, and Ritchie Lowry for their suggestive comments and criticisms at various stages of my research, and Dolores Kronberg for her highly competent secretarial aid and typing.

Max L. Stackhouse
July 1970

Preface

During the past several years, there has been an intense political, economic, and moral debate about the existence and character of the "Military-Industrial Complex." The phrase is used as a negative moral term by those who oppose major features of American foreign policy and our domestic political-economic modes of organization. And, among the politicized protestors of Viet Nam, the definitions have become slogans automatically referring to a militaristic power elite that is both a manifestation of neo-imperialism abroad and an agent in corrupting the American dream at home. If critics are pressed, however, they often acknowledge that the whole thing is more complicated than that. But they continue to claim that, as a symbol, the phrase *Military-Industrial Complex* points to something fundamental and something fundamentally wrong about the shape of the United States today. Those who approve of the basic directions of our policy or polity tend not to use the term or they tend to challenge the sloganeering definitions of the critics in ways that avoid their adversaries' moral questions.

The purpose of this book is to investigate the meaning of the term *Military-Industrial Complex* to find out whether the phrase and its definitions point to something real and morally dangerous and, if so, what can and ought to be done about it. Definitions that have become slogans are a variety of public, profane symbol. They therefore have all the problems of interpretation that attend symbolic language. They are rooted in some actual or presumed social-historical experience. They provide an angle of vision or stance toward that experience. They have both emotive and rational elements. They identify or point toward certain dimensions of human experience that are seen as decisive for good or ill. They have hidden in them at least implicit indications of what the means of access to the good or the remedies for the ills are. And they presume to relate or point to some ultimate frame of reference by which the interpretations are legitimated. The Military-Industrial Complex, thus, is a value-laden social symbol that invites both empirical and moral analysis.

There are two contexts that inform this study. First, in contrast to many who write on the Complex, I do not come to the study of the topic primarily through anti-war activities. This effort is not, as it were, a "movement" document. While sympathetic to a good bit of the anti-Viet Nam protest, my own concern and study have been in the areas of urban problems and minority groups. I have been trying to understand the moral foundations of large-scale institutions, particularly as they appear in modern metropolis. What are the ethics of complex organizations, and how do they shape, support, or destroy people, genuine religion, and civilization? It is through wrestling with this question I became aware, for a multitude of reasons that I hope will become clear, of the incapacity of this nation to solve its urban problems without paying serious attention to the Military-Industrial Complex.

The other context of this study is religious social ethics. There are three reasons for working on this problem in such a context: First, while *ethics* has many subdivisions and schools of thought, *religious social ethics* does attempt to provide an evaluative interpretation of social-historical experience from the perspective of some holistic frame of reference. Such a phenomenon as the Military-Industrial Complex requires a holistic perspective. Second, the social life of mankind and the survival of any meaningful religious life demand more intensive investigation of the meanings of those definitions that become slogans, the common symbols of secular sensibility, so that we do not live by the drift of clichés. We must try to relate the social problems we confront to the moral possibilities we envisage in a way that enriches the quality of our conventional wisdom and the range of our horizons. And third, many of our churches and synagogues are becoming increasingly involved in social and political problems. It is of fundamental importance that they enter these areas wisely, since the credibility of their moral witness, as custodians of the most profound values of the Western world, is at stake. The religious traditions have resources that can be brought to bear on public problems, and yet parts of the traditions must be reconstructed in order to provide moral leadership in the contemporary world.

Two large areas of concern are omitted from this study: tactics and threats. Tactical and strategic questions of individual and group action on the perspectives of this study should they be adopted are hinted at, but not spelled out. As one never convinced by the kind of objective scholarship that leads to inactive balancing of arguments, it is my hope that this effort will lead some to action and involvement. But local variables are too idiosyncratic to be specified here. As to threats, I do not think that it is necessary to deal with the Military-Industrial Complex in terms of the international threat of communism. Elementary investigation in this whole area reveals that American nuclear power is so great, so overwhelmingly great, that no present power in the world can engage in serious threats without jeopardizing its own destiny. The fact that various nations are perceived as threats says more about our perceptions than about the threats. I will, therefore, try to say something about the nature of these perceptions. Further, the Military-Industrial Complex is as much a domestic problem as it is one of international relations. It has primarily to do with the shape, relation, and combined influence of some of the decisive institutions within American society. Finally, the issues posed by the Military-Industrial Complex raise questions that pertain to all modern, industrialized societies, East or West, although our experience is peculiarly shaped by our own history.

This study, then, attempts within these boundaries to provide ethical guidance for morally concerned persons and groups trying to find a way to be responsible in the face of vast institutional structures of our society. It does not attempt to tell one how he must think, act, or vote on a specific issue that is to come before the public. But it does attempt to sensitize concerned men and women to the major dimensions of the problem

and to direct their attention to decisive areas and considerations
that affect the general shape of things. The guidance offered
here, therefore, attempts to locate the ethical questions in the
midst of social reality and to suggest moral and political directions in which to move.

The Ethics of Necropolis

CHAPTER ONE

Theological perspectives
on war and peace

The proper end of theological, social, and ethical considerations of the problems of war and the instruments of war is a just peace—*shalom*. But today, as always, violence, greed, and vindictiveness are resident in human hearts and organized into human institutions. Overt and covert injustice inhabit societies and relationships between societies even when there is relative peace. Competing hegemonies, representing competing politics, policies, and values, occasionally arrive at a standoff, variously interpreted as a balance of terror, or as a search for common interests, or as a coalition of the powerful against the weak. But most governments find it necessary to prepare constantly for war.

The Judeo-Christian tradition has most often approached living in the midst of vicious conflict with loyalty to *shalom*, a peace that passes understanding. The vision of a future where the lamb lies down with the lion and men study war no more is an essential ingredient of the religious ethics of the West, from which it has passed into the consciousness of many not self-consciously religious. Often cast in terms of hopes for the Kingdom of God or for a New Jerusalem, for a worldwide City of God or for a *polis* of transformed quality, the tradition has kept alive the human dream, and in some cases the expectation, that somehow, somewhere, wanton conflict can be mitigated. The tradition has also, however, taught us that sometimes, until the hopes of the ages are fulfilled, intentional violence may be required. Both realistic and visionary aspects inhabit this view. It presupposes that the actual state of man and the world is conflict and hostility, that conflict and hostility are often built into

social complexes which magnify them and multiply their destructive effects. It also presupposes that man can and ought to
take certain actions in order to more nearly approximate to the
justice, righteousness, joy, and love that characterize *shalom*.

The peculiar Judeo-Christian mix of realistic and visionary dimensions of life is a delicate balance which bears within
it the temptations to cut short either the visionary or the realistic
dimension. The notion that men and nations can somehow
spiritually leap out of their historical context directly into a set
of heavenly human relations on earth has been a perennial
temptation for religious utopians. While keeping alive the
vision of a new and radically transformed future for man, the
attempts to begin acting now as if that divine future were fully
upon us has led not only to the danger of moral isolation from
questions of public policy, but also to forms of pathological self-
righteousness within the religious community when its parochial
claims were ignored by the community at large. And in those
few instances where the visionary dimensions became so influential in public policy that the government recoiled from the use
of power, exterior destructive powers threatened the very existence of the community itself. (note 1) Both in the United States
and in England, for example, liberals refused to face the implications of the rise of Hitler. If, however, the contrary dimension
of the tradition is accented to the detriment of any visionary tension toward the future, the realist easily becomes the cynic. No
residues of human hopes and aspirations, no sensitivity to the
beliefs, values, and intimacies that constitute the tissue of life
are taken into account in the skeletal calculation of who can
deploy the largest army. When warned of the power of the
Vatican, Stalin is reputed to have asked, "How many divisions
has the pope?" The memory that victors write history in terms
of their victories is invoked as the clinching argument that our
resources must be marshaled for the inevitable violence. The
moral tradition is studded with examples of the dual pathologies
of being simply visionary or simply realistic.

But the peculiar and delicate balance of the Judeo-
Christian mix has been as often distorted by its alliances with
other polarities in the debates over war and peace, isolation and

international relations. The mix has been successively adulterated by identifying too fully with liberal or conservative political ideology alone in some periods and by stating its case in naturalistic or idealistic terms in others.

By *liberal*, I mean a tendency to accent the potential good in the individual. Through the efforts of individuals, whether by acts of spontaneous will or calculated rationality, society can turn a new corner in human affairs which will make the future discontinuous with the unfortunate past. By *conservative*, I mean the tendency to accent the corruption of man and the potential evils of departing from the tried and true ways of social cohesion. Man's rootage in the past preserves him from the chaos of his own presumptuousness about shaping his future. By *naturalist*, I mean the recognition that man is a creature, rooted in the processes of the biophysical universe, and that therefore his instincts, impulses, and interests are decisive. By *idealist*, I mean the recognition that man can, by communicating ideas through the pulpit, lectern, or forum see new horizons and reconstruct his social life. Man is a creator as well as a creature and can build civilizations on values that transcend the natural needs and processes of existence. The interaction of these basic divisions in the way people think about the world often produces moral conviction and stance. But it also engenders four basic quasi-theologies that are the perennial temptations of the tradition which need to be clarified and set aside at the outset. They are in fact quite sophisticated modes of thought, but they too have their own popular slogans that indicate peculiar angles of vision on the Military-Industrial Complex.

Many morally concerned social critics have kneaded into the inherited mix, liberal and naturalistic notions that can only be called, in combination, romantic. The romantics hold that wars are fought by the generals and not by the peoples themselves. Were men left free from the machinations of politicians and professional soldiers, wars would not occur. "Suppose," says the poster, "they gave a war and nobody came." Natural man weaves the social fabric through his spontaneous affinities for and natural ability to get along with his fellows.

"Make love not war." If people are only allowed to be themselves, the devastating effects of artificial, mechanical, bureaucratic super-structures would be automatically avoided and people would be more human. Man is good. Governments make wars. Sin is institutionalization. Salvation is achieved by the destruction of the institutions that are the sources of repression. "Void where prohibited." Social and cultural forms by their very nature threaten the noble savage and diminish his capacity for fulfilling his personhood.

Universalistic liberals, by contrast, do not call for the abolishment of governmental or societal forms, not even of those which prepare for conflict and war. Instead, they call for the immediate construction of an ever-larger supergovernment within the nation as a stepping stone to an international one that can exercise restraint against competing nation states. "World Peace through World Law." The ideal is a great new Athens of the world. On idealistic grounds they hold that the establishment of world government through institutionalizing universal values would provide a legitimate and legitimizing system of norms for controlling all conflict and hostilities. "Support Your United Nations." Natural man may well be nasty, brutish, and mean; but under the impact of a cosmopolitan urbanity developed through international dialogue he is simultaneously capable of developing a system of institutionalized norms that control the destructive propensities of men and nations. "This year, invite your foreign friends to visit America."

Although the romantics recognize the necessity for primary expression, and the universalists the necessity for artificial institutions and intercultural dialogue to preserve civilizing moral and legal norms, they both fail to sustain the mix of the visionary and the realistic that is present in the Judeo-Christian tradition. The romantic fails to recognize the intrinsic connections between the private concerns and interests of persons, and the governmental structures they develop or permit. Corruption of men and institutions is a two-way traffic and neither is primordially innocent. The universalist fails to recognize that we do not have structures which could prevent a world government from becoming a greater hegemony of the powerful over the weak within one uncontrovertible system. The best structures of human law are indeed a guide to the good, but they also inevitably reflect the rationalizations and group egoisms of those who make them, and they fail to sustain the visions for transformation that reach beyond present conflicts.

	naturalist	idealist
liberal	romantic	universalist
conservative	localist	reactionary

Figure 1. American ideological biases

The conservatives fare no better. Naturalistic conservatives accent the necessity for primary, small-group, and local brotherhoods as the only genuine arenas where reality can be found. Large bureaucracies, grandiose ideas, vast cultural forces stretching across national boundaries and across time are so diffuse as to be empty. Man lives in specific and concrete matrices of interests and affections. Pagan localism becomes the "natural theology" and theory of the good. If one is dealing with community problems, the family is seen as decisive; if one is dealing with state issues, the local community is the center of loyalty; if one is dealing with national issues, "states rights" is the appeal, and if one is dealing with the world situation, the present nation-state is the criterion of righteousness and patriotism the highest virtue. "America: Love it or Leave it." The divinely created order and the immediate structure of the given community become identified. In international relations one can only deal with realistic policy by calculating the national self-interest. The cause and the cure of problems are ever referred to the more local particularity, with *our* particular matrix seen as a manifestation of the good, at least for us, and *theirs* or *other's* seen as threatening. It is "natural" and realistic for us to fight for "ours" and others to fight for "theirs." It is part of the scheme of things, and we must fight all the harder to preserve this order against the artifacts of woolly-minded liberals who want to turn it over to any "them" or move in some fuzzy altruistic direction. Indeed, such attempts are usually rationalized masks for the self-interests of certain groups anyway.

Idealistic conservatives depend not so much on deriving normative categories from an empirical observation about man's "natural" parochial loyalties as from an attempt to reactivate ideals and principles out of the past. Dedication to "Capitalism and The Ten Commandments," says the masthead of a conservative newspaper, has made this nation what it is. The preservation of an independent spirit requires a constant vigilance against those who oppose our freedom or who tamper with previous interpretations of eternal values. Therefore we must constantly guard against, and constantly prepare for threats to, our moral and spiritual values while we hold firmly to the eternal principles for which we stand. Our weapons are legitimate instruments for the enforcing of Truth against those loyal to Falsehood.

While the localists preserve the sense of vitality that provides meaning and security to millions and while the reactionary reminds us of the inevitable continuities of history and of the impossibility and undesirability of forsaking values our forefathers died for, the small-mindedness of the localistic and the rigid myopia of the reactionary conservatives end in a parochialism of loyalties that both obscures and preserves the present situation. Both varieties of conservatism ultimately fail, the localist because forces that affect human life are in fact broader and deeper than those present in particularities, and the reactionary because it leads to a paranoid hard-heartedness that constricts the human vision by only looking backward. From the standpoint of the Judeo-Christian mix of realism and idealism, the former conservatism smacks of polytheistic idolatry of every locale where some vitality is present, and the latter conservatism grasps none of the vision of a divine future, only a mythological memory of a divine, but fallen past.

The interpretation of human arenas of violence by the more cogent representatives of the Judeo-Christian tradition cuts across ordinary divisions of naturalism and idealism as they appear in the uneasy alliances* of liberal or conservative ideology in the United States. The Judeo-Christian tradition cannot therefore deal with war and peace by reference to political ideologies alone. Although its realism demands that it find its way in the midst of present political possibility, its perspective on human affairs in regard to international conflict rejects the oversimplifications that continually unbalance its mix of the visionary and the realist. Instead, the tradition demands an ethical analysis of the human, social, and cultural forces that cause our present dilemmas, recognizing that we cannot once and for all put an end to human perversity and conflict, but demanding that we analyze the situation in such a way that the pressure points for mitigating those propensities are exposed. Such an analysis may well require modified insights from the various current political ideologies, but it cannot enter into an uncritical alliance with any one of them.

The Judeo-Christian tradition claims to provide insights that allow a distinctive and penetrating definition of the context of human existence, and to provide some of the normative guidelines for dealing with that context. Under the impact of the notion of a God who enters into the grit and grime, struggles and celebrations of an Exodus community and who became again concrete in the suffering, struggling community in an obscure corner of the Roman Empire, the tradition directs man's attention to an analysis of the human situation wherein conflicting norms, competing definitions of power and worth, and

---

* And they are indeed uneasy. The naturalists of both liberal and conservative stripe presently find common cause in moves toward a neo-isolationism, and they struggle together in campaigns for local control of schools and for conservation. The idealists cooperate in calling for the domestic rule of law and orderly procedure and in working out agreements in international trade.

contending structures of human relations are bumping up against one another, so that he might discern what spirits and what powers are at stake in these conflicts, sanction those that both grasp the actualities of the situation and that provide the momentum to engage in the transformation of or critical overcoming of those that destroy the possibility of *shalom*. Some of the tools of this tradition are well developed and can be stated rather clearly. Some, however, are not at all clear in the present context and will require more extensive reflection. What is relatively easier to state, may well be stated first.

The Judeo-Christian interpretation of war and peace hangs on several dimensions of human experience. These relations are expressed traditionally in metaphorical language, a language held suspect in much contemporary scholarship. Yet if we see traditional language as "the synthesis of several complex units into one commanding idea not by analysis, nor by direct statement, but by sudden perception as an objective relation," (note 2) we can grasp the ethical, social, and theological dimensions of accumulated moral wisdom more quickly.

Of primary importance is the relationship of man with God. Man's first loyalty must be to that which is ultimately powerful and ultimately valuable. Man does not know precisely what this is, yet he is called to focus primarily on that center of power and value, for it impinges on our lives in unavoidable ways. It seeks us out when our plans to assure power and worth are shattered. Man seeks it whenever he seeks power, meaning, and purpose. Throughout the testimony of scripture and tradition, man finds suggestions, characterizations, and symbols of that which is called God. And very often that center is discerned as being concrete not only in highly personal and intimate ways, but also in national and international conflict or in political structures that promote just peace.

This God of the tradition is seen as being the center of worth and power because, ultimately, only that which transcends our control can prevent ultimate destruction; only God can save. But it is not only a power that can prevent destruction, it is a center that is worthy of loyalty, for it sustains and extends goodness. Power is, at the highest level of Judeo-Christian conceptualization, linked with worth. Goodness without power is naive and empty; power without goodness is a vicious tyranny.

The significance of this fundamental relationship to God is fourfold. First, it relativizes all proximate goods and powers. No real or imagined center of value or power is worthy of primary loyalty except that which man does not and cannot possess. In the final analysis each attempt to provide foolproof security by accumulation of power, and every effort to make the ultimate values concrete, is seen as an arrogance of power and a moral pretense. No social system is beyond criticism. No national accumulation of the majesty of power and no national claim to worth is capable of assuring man of meaningful existence. Modern man may understand this assumption quite clearly, but he has not always done so. Criticism of or even failure to show proper respect for tribal, national, or cultural gods and their social forms has more often than not been the warrant for execution. Freedom to criticize the principalities and powers has derived always from the idea of a relationship to a worth and a power more fundamental than obtains in any society.

At the same time, relationship with God implies responsibility for discerning where, in the midst of life, the relative degrees of worthy power are. Man must in the face of this relationship identify and endorse those kinds of relative worth and power that preserve the possibilities of meaning and purpose and he must organize life around them so that persons and societies can withstand the pretentious assaults of spurious worth and of arrogant power. Thus, man must engage in the precarious task of constructing, sustaining, or reconstructing social matrices which can bear significant human meanings and purposes. The Christian tradition has specified these in terms of the trinity, a concept developed, as we shall note in a later connection, when early Christianity confronted imperial power in a particularly virulent form. Considered from a social-theological perspective, the three-in-one concept suggests that the decisive social matrices are: The Fatherhood principle of righteous order, the Sonhood principle of whole identity, and the Spirit principle of enthusiastically and freely covenanted community. (note 3) In the concrete experience of these possibilities, the vision of *shalom* in the midst of tragic reality becomes concrete.

Third, the theological metaphor of the trinity suggests that the fundamental and normative kinds of relationships for men are many. Precisely because the ultimate center of worth and power is beyond human attainment and, indeed, comprehension, no single form of existence is unqualifiedly valid. Man and God are understood in relational terms, both in the claim that man has no meaningful existence outside of his relationship to God and neighbor, and that, indeed, God and his power are also pluralistic and relational in form. Therefore, monolithic hegemonies that do not preserve significant relational existence and do not admit of the possibilities of pluralism at the highest levels of society and culture are dangerous threats to any adequate understanding of man, society, or politics.

The metaphor of the relationship to God is linked to a fourth dimension of human experience: the necessity for a constructive stance, a future-oriented position. It is true that *shalom* does not presently obtain and that we only know righteous order, whole identity, and community of covenantal sharing in fragmented and therefore visionary or metaphorical ways; yet man is always given some possibility of responding in the midst of tragic destruction and conflict in a way that identifies worthy power and approximates a future where the vision can become more actual. He always finds resources of untapped worth and of power for righteousness sake that prevent cynicism or despair. He confesses, ultimately, to an undying optimism that mitigates the necessary penultimate pessimism, for life is rooted in a power and worth that can never be exhausted by pretended structures of power and worth. And out of this tradition, over the centuries, three major options have grown: Holy War, Pacifism, and Just War. (note 4)

Holy War is a kind of intentional group violence that attempts to destroy clear and present evil in order to preserve a righteous order against the chaos of aggressive threats or to establish a new order out of destructive chaos by the moral use of the sword. Having precedence in Biblical literature, Islam, the Crusades, and the Radical Reformation of the sixteenth and seventeenth centuries, and finding fresh approval in both modern revolutionary theory and counter-revolutionary "preventive warfare," Holy War presupposes an apocalyptic confrontation of good and evil that must be faced now. The future is upon us. Survival and salvation depend upon the immediate victory of the righteous against the evil forces. The relation to the future is collapsed into the present, for the future is decided by loss or victory in the present.

Although the Judeo-Christian tradition has been involved in Holy War at various times, it has always had serious reservations about it. Theologically, there is too great a temptation to assume that power and worth are in fact totally on "our" side; there is no critical distance, no relativizing of the institutions and values which presently exist. Further, the frenzy of wrath that attends Holy War is so total that it destroys those fragile matrices of relative worth and power which provide foundations for the current vision of ultimate worth and power. The consequences, then, of Holy War are idolatry or cynicism and unmitigated destruction. And socially, Holy War has nearly always been so mixed with one or another form of liberalism or conservatism that it was unable to avoid their respective reductionisms. Holy War often turned the liberal or conservative parties toward romantic or reactionary orgies of devastation. Hence the Judeo-Christian tradition has never been able to endorse Holy War without serious qualification.

Under the impact of nuclear weaponry, the possibility of Holy War has been further reduced as a moral option. Although previous Holy Wars were fantastically destructive relative to the dimensions of the societies in which they occurred, the ideological totalism of Holy War was marginally possible when material possibilities of total destruction were impossible. But when the capacity for total destruction came on to the horizon with the geometric increase in accessible material power, the ideological possibility of such totalism had to be challenged. The imminence of power forced concentration on the transcendence of legitimate claims to the right to use it. Only God may destroy utterly; and no nation, no people has exclusive claim to usurp God's freedom. Therefore, almost all contemporary ethicists rule out Holy War or at least nuclear Holy War as a live option. (note 5)

There is one area, however, where Holy War short of nuclear war is preserved as a moral possibility, in spite of its apocalyptic dangers. There is a possibility of a "righteous revolution." That is, when "law and order" becomes systematized repression and organized chaos; when lies and inhumanity put on the mask of truth and humanitarianism; when political, economic, and spiritual exploitation prevent any peaceful pattern of change and reform, there is a moral obligation to establish a new order of justice and righteousness, by violent means if necessary, in the name of all that is holy. Walter Rauschenbusch stated the case three quarters of a century ago. After arguing for the moral superiority of peaceful resistance, he asked,

> But what if peaceful redress is denied? What if . . . the public voice is stifled, even the humblest petition draws down cruel punishment on the petitioners, and the aspirations of patriotism and popular devotion, which would be the pride of other countries, are treated as crimes? What if in the struggle of an oppressed class for its rights the oppressor should pack juries, procure special legislation, mislead public opinion by corrupting the press, slander the champions of the poor, and in every way defeat the legitimate efforts for justice? . . . What if some state should one day appear not to be the organized people at all, but an organized class rebelling against the unorganized people? (note 6)

In such a situation, the moral possibility of Holy War in the specific and limited meaning of righteous revolution remains alive. At times, it forms a coalition with romantics who "feel in their gut" that there is no hope for the present establishment, and that to be faithful to true human conditions, guerrilla warfare is called for. Often it becomes the ally of universalistic liberals who long for a new "super-order" on "liberated terms" that will prevent all forms of military, social, and cultural imperialism. It also, however, frequently has to make an alliance with localist conservatives of a nationalistic bent who demand local sovereignty in all situations. And, on occasion, it becomes linked with reactionary ideologues in discussions of the moral righteousness of "preventive intervention," or "anticipated counter-insurgency bombing" to preserve our values before potential evil becomes strong enough to threaten.

Despite the many possible alliances of righteous revolutionary sentiment, which make it highly unpredictable, an interesting moral shift takes place in the move from Holy War to righteous revolution. For a series of criteria gradually manifest themselves, by which, even if they are varied and unsystematically presented, one may judge the propriety of the righteous revolution, and which place the burden of proof that the situation requires it upon the righteous revolutionary. Holy War as a direct command of God can no longer be claimed. Instead, one looks at the human, historical, and social situation to see whether a righteous revolution is demanded. One is forced to acknowledge that there are moral limits and empirical conditions under which violent action may be required, possible, or desirable, and under which, by the same token, it may not. Thus, it becomes necessary to articulate the criteria by which such situations are judged and to analyze the situation closely to see if the criteria are met.

The second possible stance in the history of the Judeo-Christian tradition is *Pacifism.* Under the influence of the eschatological ethic that dominates large sections of the New Testament and some segments of the Jewish traditions, Pacifists attempt to anticipate, in immediate personal and group life, the future life of just peace, love, and righteousness. Symbolically enacting in the present the future harmony of man, they engage in a literal actualization of the vision of *shalom.*

The perfectionism or utopianism that is required to sustain the Pacifist orientation more often than not drives such a group into a sectarian position against society. Thus, it tends to develop an anti-establishment stance that allows it to merge with the secular romantics. One sees precisely such an alliance in the recent affinities between the peace churches and many of the secular war resisters in this country. At the same time, the perfectionism demands a firm adherence to the preservation of traditional principles, allowing in some respects, an alliance with idealistic conservatives. Thus, for example, Pacifism is maintained by some very conservative Jewish and Christian Biblical literalists and by non-church commentators who hold that the religious tradition, if it is to be believed at all, must be held as rigid adherence to an absolute principle of love that would refuse to kill anyone under any conditions. Congressional conservatives in this country have allowed legal provision for absolute Pacifism to pass without serious obstacles, although they vigorously oppose any form of conscientious objection that is not based on such perfectionism. They drive a wedge between the visionary and the realistic dimensions of the Judeo-Christian tradition and forbid them to be a part of the same mix. These conservatives permit a moral leap to the eschatological perfection of the future so long as one does not try to wed it to political, social, and economic realities or to inform one's moral judgment by political, social, and economic considerations. The necessary realistic distinctions between historical states of affairs—some of which may require force, some counterforce, and some passive resistance to force—are seen to be empty. Some Pacifists accept the disjunction between matters of faith and matters of this world and claim that such a disjunction is precisely what the tradition is about. Others, more pathetically, believe that Pacifism is a powerful weapon, a technique, available to the wise or the faithful which could, if only exercised, easily defeat hostility and aggression in the human heart and in human institutions.

The Judeo-Christian tradition has always been of two minds toward Pacifism. In early periods when small minorities held to the faiths in a Greco-Roman world, the stance was widespread. And throughout history, the tradition has recognized that some with specially sensitive consciences are called to a vocational attempt to preserve the vision of *shalom* in the midst of the contentious violence that characterizes much of human existence. Therefore, Pacifism serves as a necessary counterbalance to the uncritical advocates of Holy War who leap to the fore in every crisis and to mere realism that only calculates probabilities. But wherever the tradition has had a chance to influence the responsible use of power and authority in political affairs, it has been critical of Pacifism. The tradition has, in fact, realistically denied both an absolute disjunction between spiritual and social-political matters and the relevance of Pacifism as a technique to solve problems of human nature or to sustain and protect degrees of relative justice. (note 7) One may not ethically raise a vocationally appropriate guideline for some persons to the level of an absolute principle to guide all public policy. (note 8)

As Holy War concepts were modified by the development of nuclear weapons, so Pacifist notions were also. Large numbers of moralists and concerned humanists, not previously Pacifists, moved toward a position of "nuclear pacifism." That is, they saw the possible use of nuclear weapons so horrendous in its potential to destroy any human future that they could conceive of no conditions in which such weapons could morally be used. At the same time, they realistically recognized the necessity for limited military action to prevent local disputes from growing out of control and escalating into nuclear exchange. And they recognized the necessity for relative balances of power to prevent nuclear blackmail by the strong against the weak. More traditional Pacifists also became involved in the investigation of the social and economic conditions under which violence became a matter of public policy, thereby engaging in a process of drawing links between the visionary and realistic dimensions of the tradition.

Two consequences of this move to modified pacifism are worthy of note. On the one hand, moralists were plunged into a morass of debates over whether having nuclear weapons was immoral or whether only using them was beyond the pale of moral responsibility. If a state has them, may they be used to threaten recalcitrant international offenders although there is no intention to use them? Or must the state announce that they would never be used, or that they would never be used first, or are there some kinds of nuclear weapons that could be used and others that could not, or what? At this stage, most nuclear pacifists retreated to calls for international or even unilateral nuclear disarmament depending on the degree of perfectionism that obtained in the nuclear pacifism.

On the other hand, moralists began to try to specify conditions and limits under which violence may be employed, a moral shift that moved Pacifism (as it did the concept of Holy War) toward a more realistic calculation of historical circumstance and toward a specification of the principles of justifiable use of limited violence. At the personal level, there is a growing movement in the churches to develop a concern for "selective conscientious objection" that has been endorsed by nearly all major Jewish and Christian bodies. Selective conscientious objection is the term given to that moral stance which claims the right to exemption from an obligation to fight in some wars if the war is deemed immoral, even where there is no claim to absolute Pacifism. The foundation of this effort rests in the notion that there is a positive religious moral responsibility to make relative political and social judgments and to abstain from immoral participation. And at the international level, the potential destruction of total societies forced a less sectarian orientation and demanded a kind of moral analysis that did not depend on the conversion of more and more people to the vision of a society governed only by the law of love, but was pertinent to actual problems of international statesmanship.

As with the notion of Holy War, most moralists and theologians not connected with the perfectionist, sectarian churches consider Pacifism to be immoral as an unqualified position. Nevertheless, there are limited and specific forms of Pacifism that remain viable. Some forms of vocational or nuclear pacifism attempt to preserve both the realistic and the visionary dimensions of moral responsibility on grounds of a diversity of gifts, of a necessary counterweight to perennial Holy War advocates, or of a discrimination among the necessary means for the preservation of a future possibility of just peace.

The mainstream of the Judeo-Christian tradition, however, has not relied on either Holy War or Pacifist orientation.

It has rejected these not only for the reasons mentioned above, but because to choose either option tends to be a once-for-all decision. By making a moral decision for the absolutism of either Holy War or Pacifism, one is relieved of any further moral discernment or decision-making. No further exercise of moral calculation is required. The stance is settled, and historical variation is deemed irrelevant. Covering the broad spectrum from that of the righteous revolutionary to the modified pacifist, the Judeo-Christian tradition, by and large, has increasingly called politically and socially informed those moral positions that both grasp the shifting character of violence and conflict and provide limits to them. Yet it has demanded discrimination among those positions in terms of relative degrees of justice and righteousness. The traditions offer at the same time a perspective that transcends the present and evokes action toward a more humane, indeed, a divine future. In short, the simple stances of Holy War and Pacifism have been properly compromised in favor of a position that recognizes a spectrum of possible responses to violence and war variable according to the actualities of the situation.

The situation, however, tells us very little unless it is interpreted and unless there are some guidelines by which it can be evaluated. Thus, within this spectrum there have developed two styles of moral reflection: one focused on the interpretation of the situation, and one upon the clarification of the guidelines by which the situation is to be judged. Both are properly moral, for the adequacy of the former depends upon the choice of interpretive categories which are used to identify the crucial characteristics of the situation in order to see what powers and values are in conflict and to assess their relative merit. The adequacy of the latter depends upon its capacity to clarify the principles that can serve as guides to policy. Both demand linking the visionary with the realistic, and the moral concept with empirical evidence.

The first style of ethical analysis, however, can best be understood through the analogy to social history and politics, as they interpret the conditions, motivations, and forces which move men and nations. It tends to ask, as does social history, what presuppositions, patterns of authority, and circumstances have forced men into choices between intolerable alternatives, and then, like politics, it asks how the presuppositions, structures of responsibility, and conditions can be changed to allow for more responsible freedom in decision and action. Frequently, this mode of moral reflection attempts to shape society's perception of reality and thereby develop a sufficient body of commitment and consensus that can deal with social-political dilemmas. Society is forced to realize (most often, unfortunately, through the onset of a crisis) that the current situation is intolerable, and it then becomes more receptive to analyses and proposed solutions it might not otherwise accept. In 1932, for example, economic ideas that had been discussed and rejected for years were successfully used by Roosevelt to inaugurate the New Deal. Public acceptance, under the impact of the depression, was virtually nationwide. The moral problem, in this view, depends upon perception, decision, and the level of the "conventional wisdom" of the people as much as it does on precise rational use of principles. At its best, nevertheless, it is not antirational or anti-principial. Rather, it understands ethical problems to be at least in substantial measure a problem of ethos which includes the interplay of symbolic and social forces that define the boundaries of human decision-making and public policy.

While more of the intellectual and ecclesiastical leaders of the Judeo-Christian tradition have attempted this style of ethical analysis, the other variety is better developed. Not only does the above model offer temptations to the worst forms of journalism and crisis reportage, but the social and political sciences which can properly inform the effort have a shorter history than the disciplines that inform the second option. The style of the latter appears most clearly in analogy to law and jurisprudence. Jurisprudence and the study of law clarify in abstract or casuistic fashion the principles or hierarchy of values that can serve as guides to policy and in the judging of relative claims. This style is deeply rooted in the moral tradition as it was already developing prior to the rise of modern historical consciousness and democratic ideals of community participation in decision-making. Its long tradition, therefore, allows particular moral dilemmas to come under the scrutiny of long established principles, and tends to ask what hierarchy of values ought to be brought to bear on a situation by those in responsible positions.

The chief legacy of the latter style of moral reflection in matters of war and peace is the ancient Just War doctrine. Brought back into the forefront of contemporary moral reflection by the voluminous writings of Paul Ramsey, (note 9) the notion is an attempt to clarify the principles that ought to be brought to bear in considering both the moral possibility of war and the kinds of means that may be morally employed in the conduct of war. The doctrine has been stated in numerous forms since the rise of Constantine brought the Christian traditions face to face with the obligations to give moral guidance on social-political matters and it has deeper roots in both ancient Jewish literature and Stoic political philosophy. In its many forms, it provides a check-list of what conditions have to be met before intentional violence may be carried out. Violence, killing, and war unleash such demonic forces that the burden of proof is upon any who claim their right to use them. But the perversity of man's inhumanity to man makes sustained use of these sometimes necessary in order to preserve life, community, and some modicum of justice and order. Thus the tradition stands against Pacifism in that it presupposes that killing is not the only wrong, and no single moral commitment can account for the variety of norms that must be brought to bear on matters of statecraft. Man does have the obligation to preserve human life, but that also implies protecting the weak against the exploitation by the strong. And there is also the obligation to preserve a quality of life that sustains and extends that life. And when destructive forces are loosed in the human arena that destroy either the *esse* or the *bene esse* of human existence they must be opposed realistically. In these cases, it is morally possible that intentional killing may be the lesser wrong or a positive obligation even though it is intrinsically evil. The doctrine also seeks to find more universal criteria than the political or social sentiments

of a particular group or the relative righteousness of a particular
cause. Hence it stands in contrast to most claims to patriotic
or religious Holy War and demands that such claims be subject to the broader judgments of human wisdom developed
by normative reflection in theology, philosophy, and international jurisprudence to limit and restrain war and preserve
some possibilities for just peace. But it also acknowledges conditions under which both righteous revolution and tactical
pacifism may be required.

I have found the following ten conditions the most useful summary of the crucial implications of the Just War doctrine.
Intentional violence is evil, but justifiable use of war and the
instruments of war may occur when and if:

1. It is a *last resort*. When other attempts to control
obvious evil and destruction have been exhausted and have
failed, the control of the forces of destruction by force may be
required. But other means must have been attempted. The God
who is Lord is first of all a God of love and peace, but in the
face of rampant evil, he is also a God of judgment.

2. There is a *just cause*. The purpose of a party trying
to correct evil or establish righteousness must not only be
claimed, but must be shown to be right by making a credible
case that freedom, equity, and order are being undercut by a
potential enemy and that they will be secured by the proposed
action. The Lord is a God of justice for which freedom, equity,
and order are regulatory principles.

3. It is carried out by *legitimate authority*. Just War
norms are political norms and are to be carried out by legally
constituted offices of government, although that may vary from
appointed to elected representative officers. Most contemporary
moralists hold that such officers must adequately represent the
will of an informed population as decided by constitutional
process, although some who are close to the "righteous revolutionary" position mentioned above see the "will of the people"
as the sole criterion of legitimacy. (note 10) The covenants
which bind man to man in social-political communities are to be
honored, for man under God is a relational being.

4. There is a *hope of success*. Men and nations have a

responsibility to be prudential in their calculation of the possibilities and consequences of attempts to displace evil and to establish righteousness. There is no room for fanaticism, or adventurism in matters of such moment. The assumption of moral responsibility that may require destruction of other persons demands clear-headed moral sobriety.

5. *More good than harm* will come from the action taken. One does not engage in an expenditure of resources of men and material that deprives other areas of human society of their just needs, creating new evils as vicious as the old.

And there are governing principles to cover the means that may be employed if violent action, on the above criteria, is judged to be permissible. In war one must:

6. *Announce the conditions* under which war would occur and publicly declare a state of hostility and the justification for it when it does occur. A due regard for the moral sentiment of mankind, including the enemy, requires that public business be conducted publicly.

7. *Attempt to discriminate* between combatants and non-combatants. Innocent parties, such as women, children, or politicians attempting to construct a just peace in the midst of conflict, must be left out of the conflict. They may not be used as shields or intentionally harmed. Those who are not bearers of the evil being destroyed must be protected from both the evil and the efforts to combat it.

8. *Use force proportionate* to the power of evil. No human community is so perverse that it has no redeeming features. And the instruments of violence are so horrendous that they must be kept under control. Thus unconditional surrender or "burning a house to kill a mouse" are ruled out.

9. *Match* an attack on an evil force by an *attack on conditions*, social, economic, political or whatever, that caused or contributed to or allowed that force to develop. There is today sufficient awareness of the way in which injustice and want breed greater injustice and destruction. Traditional Just War concepts (which do not explicitly include this provision) might well be expanded to include an effort to combat the contributing causes of evil as a necessary part of the means in com-

bating evil. A necessary commitment to destruction must also entail a commitment to reconstruction. And, finally,

10. *Treat the enemy with mercy.* The wounded, the captive, the defeated, are part of humanity and no longer in a position to bear the force of evil and destruction against which justifiable violence is exercised. Hence, they are to be treated as brothers. (note 11)

The clarification of such principles is a necessary part of the ongoing task of ethics and they are presumably applicable to all parties concerned. No party or nation is without guilt on one or several of these norms in situations of conflict. But relative approximation to them is required. Such provisions demand that those defending or protecting policies look at many related sides of a question before advocating the intentional use of violence. Such provisions also demand analysis of the empirical situation at every point. They provide normative categories that are useful in a wide range of situations. And they systematize public debate over specific issues. Indeed, appeal to such principles appears to be unavoidable even among those who reject Just War theory. In every argument I have seen short of Holy War patriotism or absolute Pacifism, for example, on the morality or immorality, legality or illegality, wisdom or folly of Viet Nam, these are the issues of debate. (note 12)

But the style of doing ethics—of refining one's principles—embodied in the Just War approach is not above criticism. It ignores some dimensions of the realistic-visionary stance between "righteous revolutionary" and "modified pacifists." It tends to focus on principles governing policy, thereby neglecting the *polities* which make policy. Yet there is strong evidence that the structure and authority of decision-making groups are themselves influential in what facts are perceived as decisive and what patterns of conventional wisdom are decisive in the application of norms to situations. And, as nuclear armament demanded a modification of Holy War theory and of Pacifism, so the broad middle range of Just War reflection might well be subject to revision in the face of the power of modern decision-making institutions with regard to war and peace. Unfortunately, the alternative ethical style, which accents ethics more in the manner of social history and politics than of law, that style which might contribute most to supplementing the more principalist approach, is not so well developed. The vast literature of this style on issues of war and peace is scattered, *ad hoc,* often sermonic or journalistic, sometimes propagandistic, and, when sustained and serious, heavily dependent on the personal brilliance or intuitive capacities of the authors (as with Reinhold Niebuhr). It cannot, therefore, be easily, or in many cases, fruitfully, summarized or recapitulated. Yet some dimensions of the present ethos require normative social-political analysis; these dimensions determine the moral responsibility for limiting war and attaining a just peace, but they do not fit neatly into the criteria developed by Just War theory. Ideological presuppositions and structural conditions are inextricably linked with the matrix of weapons research, development, production, installation, delivery, and the interpretation of empirical information. Definitions of what or who constitute "evil forces" and "the enemy" determine our perceptions of just cause and legitimate authority or relative goods and relative harms. All of these raise morally valid questions as to the long-range consequences of an extensive set of links between the inevitable military and industrial and educational institutions in all modern nuclear societies. On these questions, Just War theory and the principalist style in general provide us with little moral guidance.

It can, to be sure, address certain questions in this realm. In the United States Senate debates over whether to deploy the ABM system or not, for example, one finds constant appeal to a number of the Just War principles. The defenders see the ABM as a bargaining device to use in negotiations, thereby *avoiding last resort responses* and establishing other mechanisms to control possibilities of destruction. The opponents seriously question the *hope of success* and whether it does entail *more good than harm.* The decision not to deploy the ABM near the cities was due to a citizen outcry that said such deployment would not allow *discrimination* in weapons exchange. (note 13)

Also, some issues of debate in the social-political area

could easily be dealt with by the rational-legal style of ethics, through other sets of principles, but not specifically by the Just War criteria. For instance, questions of cheating and padding contracts, questions of unjust if legal profits by military or industrial personnel, questions of undue exercise of special influence or indirect bribery, and similar clear cases of dishonesty, usury, and disguised grand theft are all within the purview of the principalist style of ethics. Some highly principled public leaders are beginning to expose these aspects in the military and in the relationship of corporations to military spending for modern weaponry.

But there are social-political dimensions entailed in the popular, morally pejorative term *Military-Industrial Complex* that are of fundamental social and ethical import and of long-range consequences in matters pertaining to the reality of human conflict and the vision of a just peace, but are not malleable to the touch of the analytical tools of Just War theory nor governed by the norms of the Just War stance. It is these dimensions that are the primary concern of this study, a study that will demand an excursion into areas not often touched by systematic ethical analysis.

CHAPTER TWO

Competing definitions of the military-industrial complex

The term *Military-Industrial Complex,* first used in 1960 in Eisenhower's often quoted last speech to the nation as President, has become a household word, a symbol that claims to point to an empirical reality and to present an evaluation of certain threats to fundamental values and institutions. But there is little clarity as to what the term refers to and what, precisely, the values and institutions threatened by it are. Our prime responsibility, then, is to try to sort out the ways in which the term has been used, to look at the social-historical experience that it points to, to evaluate the stances that are implied in its usage, and to analyze what values are implicit in that usage.

First, the various usages of the term should be divided between those who immediately incorporate the term into their own political ideologies and those who try to investigate the nature of the phenomenon. Of course, all commentators attempt to collect a body of documentation to support their use of the term and all are influenced by their presuppositions. But some immediately see the symbolic overtones of the term as supporting or threatening what they already hold to be true, while others attempt to link systematic analysis of the phenomenon with an interpretation of the causes and structure of institutions of war in the national and international arena.

Eisenhower's own usage of the concept apparently falls partly in the former group and partly in the latter. The core of that speech follows.

This conjunction of an immense military establishment and a large arms industry is now in the American experience. The total influence—economic, political, even spiritual—is felt in every city, every state house, every office of the Federal government. We recognize the imperative need for this development. Yet we must not fail to comprehend its grave implications. Our toil, resources and livelihood are involved; so is the very structure of our society.

In the councils of government, we must guard against the acquisition of unwarranted influence, whether sought or unsought, by the military-industrial complex. The potential for the disastrous rise of misplaced power exists and will persist . . .

Akin to, and largely responsible for the sweeping changes in our industrial-military posture, has been the technological revolution during recent decades.

In this revolution, research has become central; it also becomes more formalized, complex, and costly. A steadily increasing share is conducted for, by, or at the direction of the Federal government. . . .

The prospect of domination of the nation's scholars by Federal employment, project allocations, and the power of money is ever present—and is gravely to be regarded.

Several factors in Eisenhower's use of the term reflect the context, convictions, and presuppositions that informed him. Nearly every outgoing president in recent history has developed a concern for history: how shall his administration be viewed in the future? Was it possible that a twentieth century conservative general could set forth a retiring valedictory that would be comparable in the long run to Washington's famed remarks about "entangling foreign alliances"? There is some evidence that Eisenhower was not devoid of this sensitivity, (note 1) and that the desire for such a major statement to the people was in the back of his mind in his consultations with his special assistant and speech writer, Malcolm Moos, and his brother, Milton Eisenhower. (note 2) The result was a speech that is almost sermonic in its appeal. (note 3)

Eisenhower's frame of reference forms the second dimension of the context of these remarks. Both as President and retiring figurehead, he was informed by the notion of radically limited government. He manifested a deep concern about the morality and viability of big government, big business, big research, and big education on the contemporary scene. Something of the small-town politics and mid-west populism which shaped his anxieties finds resonance and support among both moderates and conservatives who are part of the same ethos. Thus, a latent suspicion of urban, technological society with its dependence upon vast bureaucratized forms of human relations and a moral preference for the independent entrepreneur, the self-directed inventor, and the individual scholar-researcher are part of his conservative definition of the ethos—conservative in both of the senses that he presupposed the superior moral worth of small-group relations to large ones and that he wished to reactivate the values of the past.

The third dimension of the context in which Eisenhower's warning was uttered is clearly political. Kennedy was assuming office and bringing with him a team of competent, cosmopolitan advisors who had not only made commitments to increased governmental responsibility in many areas of national welfare, but who had ridden to victory, in part, on claims about the existence of a "missile gap." Kennedy had heavily accented the clear campaign promise that large amounts of money would be allocated to military and space-research rocketry, a promise that carried encouragement for those defense industries eager to eat at the military table. Eisenhower surely was not only offering reservations about the competing styles of government and perceptions of "bigness" that were a part of the Kennedy approach, he was also denying the necessity for and pointing out the dangers of vast increases and structural integration for management in this (or, for that matter, any) area of federal expenditure. (note 4)

But in some ways his comments imply more systematic analysis. He suggests the interaction of "economic, political and spiritual" effects of the industrial-military combination, and yet he recognizes the existence of some apparently exterior threats that demand such a conjunction of military and industrial power. Further, he sees that the whole phenomenon is linked to the structures of technological development and scholarly research. Thus, what he is referring to is a very complicated set of phenomena which require close analysis to identify and interpret.

The subtleties of his suggestive remarks, however, were not always taken seriously. The term *Military-Industrial Complex* was quickly adopted as a political slogan for numerous groups. Eisenhower's words, which were both a lament for the loss of days when values and structures were not so simple and a description in telescopic form of the nature of the problem, were seldom to be the occasion for hardheaded analysis of either our values, our direction, or the specific shape of our institutions.

In many quarters, the term was immediately appropriated by the various ideological factions of the nation. The romantics saw and continue to see it as the epitome of the destructive effects of large, bureaucratic systems that repress and suppress people. The Complex is the inevitable result of the establishment. Such an appropriation of the term reigns still in large numbers of underground newspapers, especially among the youth. Liberal idealists also took the term and used it as a debating weapon to try to develop a disarmament and arms-control section of the government, under the conviction that new forms of diplomacy could bring man to more universal agreement on values and interests. Localistic conservatives also adopted the term in doubting, with Eisenhower, the capacity of large scale institutions to render any good. There are, scattered throughout the *Congressional Record* over the past decade, literally hundreds of protests, by conservative congressmen at the behest of the communities back home, about the ways bureaucratic decisions by the military disrupt the local fabric of community life and sometimes destroy the economic base of the community by closing bases or plants arbitrarily. Still other conservatives see in the Complex growing ties between government and industry which threaten the eternal truths of free enterprise and limited government. Thus, the first level of the term's appropriation has been in terms of preconceived schools of political ideology, each one of which distorts—in part because it does not really look at—the structure and dynamics of the Military-Industrial Complex of which Eisenhower spoke.

A second set of debates cuts across the above appropriations of the term. Systematic advocates of a Holy War against godless communism saw the development and employment of the term as a conspiratorial left wing attack on our fighting men. Right wing proponents of this view saw Eisenhower's employment of the term as further evidence that he was insidiously influenced by the forces of treason. More moderate militarists saw the term as just wrong-headed and began to point out the enormous controls that regulate the military and its relation to purchasing, and the large majority of national military procurement that is conducted with (at least by the given rules of the game) relative fairness. They thus denied the existence of any such Complex. The assumptions, however, that the use of the term is either a ruse for subversion or a myth with no meaning involve such presuppositions themselves that the perspectives can hardly be taken as points of departure. Nevertheless, the moderate militarists do seem to direct our attention to the fact that we cannot understand the Complex without some attention to the kinds of regulations under which military-industrial relations occur.

At the other extreme, Pacifist ideologues adopted the term as the automatic and polemical successor to a series of epithets that have been of concern throughout the twentieth century. "War Profiteer," "Merchants of Death," and "Munitions Manufacturers" had been terms of reproach for three quarters of a century. Since the Spanish-American War, and through World Wars I and II to the Asian conflicts, these terms had characterized that coterie of industrialists who had pressed for higher and higher expenditures and for more aggressive military postures abroad in the interests of higher profits. Indeed, in every period exposures of undue influence and corruption seemed to validate the Pacifist's sometimes lonely protests. Their investigations, however, fail to touch the core of what the full meaning of "Military-Industrial Complex" might be, for they tend to show it as a conspiracy of a few unscrupulous entrepreneurs. But a complex is not a profiteer, a merchant or a manufacturer or a bunch of them together. Hence it cannot be dealt with by converting them from militarism to Pacifism. It is, as Eisenhower recognized, a more subtle interplay of social and moral factors.

The Pacifists' rejection of raw power and the institutions which organize it sustain a specially sensitive conscience with regard to the expanding power of the military. They were conscious of spreading and increasingly systematic military encroachments into civilian arenas of life through the regularization of the draft, the extension of the military budget, and the apparent growing influence of the military in the nation's foreign policy. (note 5) The presuppositions of the Pacifist, however, which tend to make them view *any* move made by the military as cause for alarm, irrespective of the conditions under which it is made, render their critique suspect. Ruled out in principle is any argument having to do with the responsible use of power and the necessity of large-scale institutions for violence as a moral option under any circumstances.

Both the moderate militarists and the pacifists, the hawks and the doves, have performed a major public service by pointing out sloppy analysis on the one hand and warning of tendencies toward the garrison state on the other. Their writings and actions have often dramatically brought the problem of military-industrial relations into public view. But they have often not gone beyond the ideological presuppositions and primordial value-commitments to analysis of the link of military and industrial institutions to see what in fact the situation is. Nor have they allowed any interpretation to inform their conceptions of right and wrong with regard to institutions of war. Merely to point out from one perspective the enormity of the enemy's threat and the strangulation of efforts to meet it by petty regulations and bureaucratic controls and from another to cite the apparent pathological concern to fight and the increasing coordination of every institutional jot and tittle does not satisfy the need to find a social-political framework by which to interpret this extremely complicated modern phenomenon. Merely to assert the morality of defense against god-less forces or the immorality of violence is not helpful either. The hawks and the doves do help to keep debate alive in the political arena, but they do not provide a moral or social anal-ysis profound enough to show us why military and economic interests have taken the particular shape they have in the twen-tieth century. Nor do they provide a compelling stance to sup-plement the traditional moral criteria of the Just War theorists.

In short, both the romantic, universalist, localist, and reactionary ideologues and the religious-political absolutists have appropriated the concept *Military-Industrial Complex* in ways that are reductionistic. Therefore, their programs to deal with it are also overly simple. It has been useful, however, to attempt to identify and catalogue the chief reductionistic views by introducing some distinctions. And, with these distortions disposed of, it is possible to begin a more careful look at those who have taken the problem seriously and have tried to use some more systematic methods of investigation to grasp both what the Complex is and what if anything ought to be done about it.

The term became quickly current among several groups who had an ideological, professional, political, or economic stake in non-military policy. Professional political leaders of several persuasions, interested in honest return for the public dollar and the reduction of corporation pressure in public decision-making saw the warning as an auspicious political occasion to trim the public tax load or to find funds for progressive social legislation. They began investigations of the waste of public funds as they had during or immediately after each of the major conflicts in the twentieth century. From the "Dodge Commis-sion Report" following the Spanish-American War, through the Navy Affairs Committee hearings of the Senate at the conclu-sion of World War I, which exposed the pork barrel involved in the supply bureaus, through Senator Gerald P. Nye's investi-gation of defense profiteering in the 1930s, the actions of the Renegotiation Board established by Truman after World War II, to present exposures by Senators McClellan and Proxmire in the 1960s, one finds a succession of efforts to restrain combinations of interest from exploiting the public purse. Contemporary successors to this legacy quickly appropriated this warning as a convenient way to validate their concerns. (note 6)

It is clear from these hearings that there are interlocking communities of interest which bear enormous temptations to subvert fair contracts. The relationship between retiring military personnel and the contracting corporations is often far too intimate, although it can be argued that the skills and information gathered by a career officer are invaluable to a corporation which needs to operate and produce in a way that will mesh with government procedure and military requirements. It is also clear that new forms of contracting which involve almost continual renegotiation of the terms, cost-plus provisions, and subcontracting procurement intricacies provide a context in which the traditional moral and legal precedents are rather shaky. Finally, although it is not often in print and, as the government investigations have shown, difficult to pin down, contracting personnel from industry will privately reveal the myriad ways by which contracts are padded in order to keep marginal corporations or marginal projects in corporations alive. After all, they argue, the preservation of a team of highly skilled workers and professionals is necessary for the protection of wage earners and their families, for the future of corporations, for the maintaining of a low unemployment rate, and for the welfare of stockholders.

These hearings and investigations reveal several significant dimensions of the Military-Industrial Complex. One is the formal and informal sets of acquaintances and common interests that are established by a large negotiating-purchasing-producing process. This dimension, however, is not unique to the Military-Industrial Complex. It could perhaps be matched by the civilian dominated Highway-Oil-Steel-Auto-Industrial Complex, or the Agriculture-Food Processing-Trucking-Retail Complex, or even by the Hospital-Medical-Insurance-Drug Complex. The difference is that the Military-Industrial Complex operates almost entirely through official governmental agencies and with public funds. It therefore bears the stamp of legal legitimacy and public will which is of necessity suspicious of private influence or "special arrangements." A second dimension is the peculiar form of contracting that has developed between the military establishment and industry. A procedure that involves working out the details as you go demands constant interaction, and, even where men operate according to the rules in honor and good faith, log-rolling relationships tend to develop that surely affect the results of contract negotiations and servicing. However, when less scrupulous people become involved, influence peddling is not surprising. Finally, it is clear that providing security for one's self, family, and colleagues through securing reliable contracts from the government is linked with the motivation of national security. The coalition of such powerful sentiments tempts many to bend the rules in the midst of intense competition.

In direct contrast, however, to such investigation, a second group of scholars concerned about the Complex move in a different direction. Contemporary radical social scientists and social observers, given sociological impetus by the writing of C. Wright Mills and his disciples, attempt to recover the tradition of the "righteous revolutionary" by offering an analysis of the Military-Industrial Complex in the context of a total interpretation of American Society. Perhaps no brief document is better representative of this literature than the "New Left" monograph *Is There a Military-Industrial Complex Which Prevents Peace?* by Marc Pilisuk and Thomas Hayden. (note 7)

C. Wright Mills claims that if one analytically looks at the decisive institutional trends of society toward increased coordination and hierarchical bureaucratization, at the social similarity of those in command posts on the top of these pyramids of power, and at the extensive ramifications, to the point of totality, of decisions made at the top, one discovers a "power elite" determining the direction of the whole society. Further, this "power elite" bridges the governmental, military, industrial, and educational and communications institutions. Their authoritarian elitism tends to have tentacles of interests, especially economic, that reach throughout the world, interests that they would protect at the cost of war. Indeed, the maintaining of their power and their institutions requires a permanent war economy. (note 8)

In contrast to this point of view, a body of "pluralist" literature has built an alternative interpretation of the situation during the last decade. Backed by social theorists such as Robert Dahl and Daniel Bell, "pluralists" were explicitly critical of Mills, and held that there are multiple power blocks in the society that served as countervailing powers to prevent any single group or set of groups from such unilateral dominance. (note 9)

The analysis by Pilisuk and Hayden begins by clarifying, contrasting, and evaluating these mutually exclusive estimates. Mills' definition of power and dominance is, they claim, crude and subject to criticism on the ground that it "depicts a vital and complex social system as essentially static, as having within it a set of stable governing components, with precharted interests which infiltrate and control every outpost of decision-authority." (note 10) In fact, there is not the solidarity of power nor of interest that Mills suggests. Different arms of the alleged "power elite" pursue different goals and, frequently, their subsidiaries compete on opposing sides of public issues or foreign policy. Some benefit by expanded trade with Pakistan, some by India; some by Israel, some by Egypt; some by extension of trade agreements with Russia, some by their restriction. Dixie-crats, Harvard and Yale presidents, and General Dynamics executives are not of the same stripe. But such observations should not make us fly to the arms of the "pluralists." The "pluralists" are finally only making the rather obvious point, according to Pilisuk and Hayden, that within a common acceptance of "the American system," disparate groups are competing for advantages. And where the "pluralists" argue that civilians do control the military and that multiple groups compete for that control in a way that promotes federalistic theories of checks and balances, Pilisuk and Hayden reply that this only prevents clique dominance from becoming permanent and total.

The constant pattern in American society is the rise and

fall of temporarily irresponsible groups. By temporary
. . . [they] mean that, outside of the largest industrial
conglomerates, the groups which wield significant
power to influence policy decisions are not guaranteed
stability. By irresponsible . . . [they] mean that there
are many activities within their scope which are essentially unaccountable in the democratic process . . . No
one group or coalition of several groups can tyrannize
the rest . . . However it is clear that these groups exist
within consensus relationships of a more general and
durable kind than their conflict relationships . . . (note
11)

And this consensus is fundamentally shaped, they continue, by
the Protestant and business-oriented heritage of the country,
with its accent on free decision-making, pragmatic efficacy in
foreign affairs, private property, and a peculiar form of constitutional government. It is rooted, thus, in "core values" and
presuppositions that are directly pertinent to the social system,
for they legitimate the preservation of "private property," the
corporate economy, a particular system of partisan politics that
operates domestically, and a relatively uniform posture in foreign relations irrespective of who is in power, all of which are
to be defended by the military. "In the United States there is no
ruling group. Nor is there any easily discernible ruling institutional order, so meshed have the separate sources of elite power
become. But there is a social structure, legitimated by core values, which is organized to create and protect power centers with
only partial accountability." (note 12) And whenever one tries to
conceive of alternate strategies, alternate forms of decision making, alternate ways of approaching contemporary problems, one
bumps into one or another of the major "core values" or one or
another dimension of the social system that, backed by the
power of the military, prevents significant change in the direction of increased participatory democracy or redistributory
economics. The resulting concept, then is inextricably embedded
in the mainstream of American institutions and mores. They

hold "not that American Society contains a ruling military-industrial complex . . . [but] more nearly that American society *is* a military-industrial complex." (note 13)

The position developed by Pilisuk and Hayden appropriates the term *military-industrial complex,* thus, in a way that is quite different from that of the more "establishment" concerns of the economy-minded political professionals, as useful as they are in limited spheres. They make vivid the staggering proportions and extensive size of the military and industrial matrix that, as we shall shortly see, does indeed stun the imagination and make one recoil with the impression of wholeness. And they have attempted to offer a social-ethical use of the concept that is explicitly related to empirical, social-political analysis and to specific values. They feel the tension of the realistic and the visionary dimensions of all fundamental treatments of human affairs that pertain to war and peace. Throughout their document, the moral preferability of participatory democracy, common utilization and redistribution of wealth for the total welfare, and the prevention of international nuclear conflict stands in grim contrast to the hard-headed analysis of their likelihood. The call for a transvaluation of values and a reorganization of society catapults them into concluding discussions of society's modest prospects for conversion.

This intriguing analysis, clearly the most profound we have yet discussed, is given support by several more recent efforts in the same general direction. Gabriel Kolko's polemical *The Roots of American Foreign Policy* also sees the relationship between the Military-Industrial Complex and the overarching structures of American society, although he is quite clear that it is civilian authority and civilian-defined goals that have promoted and developed current structures and policies. He is fully aware that the military is for the most part under the control of the government at present, but sees that the widespread economic interests of America have produced a consensus as to how we relate to other nations that is now being carried out by the military through relatively democratic governmental procedures.

According to Professor John Kenneth Galbraith, (note

14) former ambassador to India, the nature of economic-techno-logical development in the United States demands the develop-ment of self-perpetuating corporations which produce a "tech-nostructure" with their own values, ideals, ideology, and defini-tion of the world. From that vantage point the managerial-technological leaders tend to make the world in their own image. That world is a conservative one, geared toward con-serving the technological-managerial systems they have built, and is presently the dominant structure in the United States. Its links with the military give it enormously enlarged power. Only by engaging in "ecumenical" political action to elect lib-erals rather than conservatives will society be able to reorient the technostructure's material priorities and thereby force a re-orientation of the corporations' material interests. Partisan poli-tics is the cure for massive "techno-structures."

David Deitch, financial columnist for the *Boston Globe* who has written regularly on this problem, sees the geometric increase of technological capacity to have far outrun society's capacity to absorb the production. Further, this production process is founded upon a class structure in which the rich get richer and the poor get relatively poorer. (note 15) Thus, it is necessary to develop some artificial means of structured waste. As Robert Gessert accurately summarizes Deitch's view, "the military-industrial complex is an enormous safety valve for our present social system against the mounting pressure of techno-logical output." (note 16) It also preserves the economic strati-fication which is necessary to preserve the technological output for the benefit of the privileged, and deflect attention from the crises of the poverty communities of the nation. Economic at-tention concentrated there would bring on a revolution that would destroy the material interests of the corporate system. Deitch too calls for partisan action, but without expressing much confidence in the prospects for change.

The most extensive and subtle of this group, however, is Richard Barnet's *The Economy of Death*. By analysis of the defense budget and the persons and institutions that manage, guide, and benefit from it, at least since World War II, Barnet comes to the conclusion that the very fabric of America is infected by a cancer within at least as dangerous as the threats from without. The political economy is caught up in a pattern of institutionalized and self-rewarding decision processes that points toward destruction. Unless this can be reversed, the nation will fail to meet its internal needs and will promote world-wide conflict. The Complex is a set of relatively integrated institutions governed by their own inner logic on the one hand (note 17) and "patrician warriors [who] are not cynics but complacent idealists," (note 18) on the other. The cure for this is a conversion process—conversion to an "economy of life." By exploring humanizing economic investments instead of programing for human destruction it is possible to develop such an economy. Barnet suggests, but does not fully elaborate on, the specifically religious and moral dimensions of this problem. He identifies part of the problem as "a new state religion of national security," (note 19) which perceives the necessity of a policy of strategic nuclear annihilation of the Soviet Union since it is "the embodiment of evil . . . too depraved to be deterred by less." (note 20)

These representative, articulate authors have several things in common. They have all attempted empirical analysis and systematic statement of decisive dimensions of the Military-Industrial Complex. They relate their analyses both to definitions of specific roles played by persons and groups and to interpretations of the overarching structures of American society. They all stand between the Pacifist and Holy War positions, some tending more toward a tactical, modified pacifism, and some toward a righteous revolutionary position. All call for political analysis and involvement as the responsibility of the people. All are offering a critique of the current operating values and ideologies of the nation as they are concretized in relationships of military to industrial institutions. These common elements make it impossible for anyone working in the area today to avoid the insight, documentation, and perspectives of these authors.

But their writings are not beyond criticism. The chief difficulty with the above perspectives, I believe, is that the authors are assuming the role of "secular preachers," and are not yet clear about that role. The real target of most of these efforts is "conversion" of the "soul" of the nation. The underlying drive is to discern and transform the "character" of the nation through "ecumenical" action. And the current debate over Viet Nam and the role of the military are the occasion for these examinations. In one sense, they have to be seen in the context of the traditions of the successive "Great Awakenings" in American history, periods in which revivalistic fervors called for new acts of piety, new personal decision-making, and new national righteousness in the face of super-personal powers. The current revival is centered in the universities rather than in the churches. As in the previous revivals, however, it is not clear that the fervor and intensity could translate into structural change or develop a socially pertinent definition of power— divine, moral, or political. The secular preachers, like their evangelistic precursors, however, do tend to generate new sectarian groups with a characteristic rejection of the sanctified establishment, and thereby raise questions about the moral foundations of present institutions.

Thus, the secular preacher can play a prophetic role. He can, indeed he must, examine the national character and point out when and where it is rooted in sin and worshiping false gods. In spite of the way preaching is so often trivialized in the churches, serious preaching is a crucial role in Western culture. The secular preachers are playing that role. But there are problems in the way they play the role in that they do not seem to be aware that they are preaching, and therefore fail to clarify certain underlying presuppositions that are required for the task. There is in all of these volumes confusion as to whether the core values of the society are defined by and ideologically invoked by the "interests" to protect the core institutions which give them control or whether the core institutions are defined by and given shape by core values, or whether there is a more subtle relationship between the two. They are caught in the dilemma of unsorted idealistic and naturalistic presuppositions. Theologically, they are not sure whether to choose Calvin or Feuerbach as their model; sociologically, they shift between the legacies of Max Weber and Karl Marx. One cannot assume that all is shaped by "needs" or "interests" if one is to be a preacher. One must assume that the transformation of values as relatively independent variables has and can shape the institutions and, indeed, the definitions of needs and interests. Preachers also must assume that the transformation of values depends in part upon the redefinition of the governing symbols and metaphors that organize man's ultimate investment of loyalties. Thus, without some attempt to attend to the development of a compelling symbolic structure, radical analysis will remain powerless and only marginally convincing. It will be tempted to see sin, but no possibilities of redemption, and hence find itself plunged either into cynicism or into developing a self-righteous set of sectarian anti-systems, directions in fact taken by many disillusioned liberals and radicals during the past few years. False gods in which people invest loyalty and potency are not displaced by the facts, but only by superior concepts of what is of ultimate worth and power.

But even at the level of social analysis, there are dimensions of the problem that the works of these authors ignore because they fail to understand the role of the preacher in the classical sense. If there is a fairly pervasive set of values and institutions coalescing in America at this time, what are its historical roots? Preachers who have tried to work with persons and institutions for the transvaluation of values and the redirection of institutions that are at least partially held together by common value commitments have found that it is a long, painful, tedious process. One has to understand how deeply rooted in history and memory the operating values and institutions are, and how much deeper one has to penetrate in order to challenge those values and institutions—unless one only wants to mobilize a mass affirmation of new faith in spectacular rallies. The Billy Graham rallies, at which the language of the nineteenth century evangelists is oversimplified, is not dissimilar from a "New Mobe" rally in which the language of contemporary secular preachers is oversimplified. Both are primarily calls to commitment and do not necessarily lead to institutional or cultural transformation.

Thus, the proposed solutions to the problem seem superficial and betray a superficial understanding of the problem in spite of the accuracy of much of the analysis. For instance, when Pilisuk and Hayden call for "convertibility of economic elites," when Gabriel Kolko claims that the chances for the American people to escape the trap of the Cold War with all its military-industrial implication depend upon the fate of resistance to the Indo-China war, or when Galbraith calls for the election of a president on this issue in the next election as the first step in the solution, one wonders whether they have been serious in pointing to the depth and breadth of the situation. Although these may indeed be bits and pieces of the solution, one wonders what the conception of the nature, power, and durability of institutional linkages actually is. In short, the tendency to describe the Military-Industrial Complex in a cross-sectional fashion tends to undercut an adequate longitudinal analysis. By looking at what it is at the moment, with only brief suggestions as to its past, it appears that it has leaped onto stage only recently and can be got off just as quickly. In fact, a good case can be made that the roots are deeper both socially and valuationally, and that any adequate response must be geared toward a long haul.

In the face of these fertile, but inadequate, appropriations of the concept of the Military-Industrial Complex, we must see how we can weave together their concerns to form a more adequate picture of what the Complex is. We will also be concerned to develop a framework of interpretation that can give us some idea of the moral issues involved in the question. The moral question, as we have already seen, is not foreign to the concerns of the various groups of observers. The political investigators of contract padding are not raising only questions of law, but questions of honesty and corruption. The pacifists see the whole struggle in terms of good and evil forces contending for control of the nation. The secular preachers, as already mentioned, are passionately concerned about the soul of the nation and the humanity of men being destroyed by arrogance and pride, egocentrism and imperialism, even if they utilize the social sciences as a vehicle for their prophecy. All end their works by calling for concerted partisan action as the course that *ought* to be taken, a moral appeal not fully acknowledged as moral by the writers themselves. The hidden moral concern of these views and their attempts to provide a realistic analysis of the empirical situation make them more penetrating than the more superficial ideological divisions of romantic, universalist, localist, and reactionary which dominate much of today's political rhetoric. They more nearly approximate the motifs one would expect to find in an analysis rooted in a conscious appreciation of the Judeo-Christian tradition. But their concerns need to be supplemented historically, theologically, and morally for their promise to be fulfilled.

CHAPTER THREE

The social sources of the complex

The Military-Industrial Complex did not leap full grown from the head of Eisenhower to become a major phenomenon of a decade's standing. It has roots in its own peculiar background and it has roots in the social history of the nation. As the defense structure of every civilization both reflects the overall shape of that civilization and bears unique features in itself, so the Military-Industrial Complex is a peculiar and concrete indicator of the larger patterns in modern America while also having distinct qualities that set it off from the mainstream of social existence. And while it is impossible to present here a complete history of the development of the Complex, an outline of its critical moments set in the context of general history is useful to an interpretation of the depth of its roots.

Throughout history, there have been at least three major types of institutions of violent human conflict. (note 1) The *primitive* war involved interpersonal combat with privately owned weapons, and it affected the total community. It was fought for the purpose of preserving the communal values, and all participants fought in the same general way. The defense of area, the preservation of women and cattle, the obtaining of women or slaves, or ritual war to prove status and fulfill cultic obligations were all means of reinforcing social solidarity and guaranteeing the continued existence of the tribal or clan community. *Historic* war, by contrast, was fought by standing armies at the behest of dukes or kings, sometimes for the sake of religious dominance—the conflict usually involving definitions of who should be proclaimed lord. Weapons were provided by specialists and clear differentiations were made between combatants and between kinds of soldiers—cavalry, archers, foot-soldiers, artillerists, etc. Otherworldly or this-worldly disputes between sovereigns were the occasion for war. *Modern* war is fought almost always between nations, and involves citizen participation led by heroic military figures. International ideology, economics, or politics becomes the primary justification for battle. Links between a professional military leadership and the industrial capacity of the nation become manifest whether the war is fought to secure raw materials and markets by conquest of colonies, to protect land and trade routes, or to extend an economic-political system.

The United States was spared combat in the international arena during most of the nineteenth century. The oceans presented natural defense barriers, and the frontiers gave open field to dissidents. Exterior enemies could not easily reach the fledgling nation and interior enemies could go west to try their hand at building something new without destroying the old, although that often involved them in primitive or historic forms of warfare against the Indian or against Mexico. Further, the vast agricultural resources allowed the people to prosper without the early movement to industrialism experienced in northern Europe. And the absence of a powerful feudal tradition allowed the Jeffersonian-Jacksonian model of citizen-soldier to remain the ideal without a large, professional, officer corps. The Protestant ethos of hard work, mastery of nature, practicality, and piety gave fuel to the burning conviction that a new social order was to develop more innocent and more virtuous than the violent and tyrannical regimes of the decadent Europe left behind, for they were constantly building modern armies to destroy each other. (note 2) But in the midst of relative national security, the economic situation of the North, the racial situation of slavery in the South and the moral indignation of the Protestant ethos shattered the pastoral exemption from large-scale conflict and plunged the nation into a civil war.

Militarily and economically, the youngest of the large nations began its trek to and through modern types of warfare into a new type. The War Between the States was won not by Lee, but by Grant, who had "spent much of his time in low-prestige quarter-master-type assignments, which were nevertheless appropriate in sensitizing him to the tasks of large-scale warfare." (note 3) The war was also won by the superior industrial capacity of the North. Given enormous stimulus by government spending during the war, the Industrial Revolution came to these shores in a sudden surge. And the Protestant ethic, which was increasingly to become wedded to notions of a divine law of evolution and the survival of the fittest, displacing previous concepts of providence, transformed the rightness of the cause into an issue involving the righteousness of God. The links between professional military leadership deeply concerned with supply and logistics, industrial leadership concerned with economic and technical aspects of production, and Protestant militance concerned with extending Yankee values were forged.

The reduction of military forces after the Civil War, however, was highly significant for the subsequent development of these links. The country was dominated by a "business pacifism that saw the development of the new found fruits of the Industrial Revolution as the harbinger of a world of plenty without war." That "business pacifism" drove the military into isolation. "Sacrificing power and influence, withdrawing into its own hard shell, the officer corps was able and permitted to develop a distinctive military character. The American military profession, its institutions and its ideal, is fundamentally a product of these years." (note 4)

The settling of the continent, the growth of industry, the development of large cities populated by a new heterogenous influx of population, and the influence of burgeoning science contributed to a transformation of American society in the last decades of the nineteenth century, plunging it necessarily into world politics and demanding reorganization of its inner structure. The nation could no longer abstain from the international arena. It was becoming too important to be left alone, and with the closing of the frontier in 1892, it looked for new horizons. Although there was no feudal base (outside the South) to be overcome, the United States increasingly began to have the same problems that attended the other major nations of the world. The transformation was capped by the Spanish-American War in which America defeated a world power and became one herself. And although it continued to conceive of itself in special terms as a "new Zion" with a "manifest destiny," America became a nation among nations.

The implications for military and industrial affairs were far-reaching. Some groups tried to preserve our Fortress America. Others tried to preserve the agrarian and commercial pacifism that had developed after the subduing of the frontier. And both tried to appropriate values from Protestantism to legitimate such efforts. Neither was possible.

The Navy had, for some time, developed a series of bureaus that had high technical skill and called for sustained professional competence. Indeed, it was the custom for the Secretary of the Navy to be a civilian ship-builder. Shipbuilding was a peculiar art that required specialized skills, and the bureaus worked closely with civilian businessmen in developing and producing these instruments of sea war. The demands for ships became more intense as the international trade of the nation developed. The application of steam power to shipbuilding transformed further the demand for skills and brought new questioning of the coordination, purpose, and scope of naval power. The establishment of the Naval War College in 1884, provided a center wherein the strongest branch of service at that time could begin to redefine itself.

Dominating the teaching of the Naval War College was Alfred T. Mahan. Writing in the midst of massive social change, he helped establish basic conceptions and directions that were to shape military development for more than half a century. A new variety of managerial and technical competence grounded in new conceptions of the military was the result.

The Navy, seen by Mahan, is the prototype of military power. It is not only concerned with national defense, it is the decisive force in world history. Trade inevitably entails a natural law of tooth and claw between contending economic forces, and sea power protects the channels for trade. Whoever controls these channels controls the destiny of national and, indeed, racial, supremacy. The ultimate purpose of the nation is expansion of economic and political power, and that can only be guaranteed by superior force. There is little to be gained by treaties and agreements, for they are unreliable when it comes to a genuine conflict of interest. Only power can adjudicate in such a situation. Thus, military power and foreign policy are of a piece, requiring a new integration of military strategy with political orientation outward. At the same time, the close interdependence between naval power and foreign trade means the developing of new links with the industrial community. (note 5)

Mahan drew many of his models and examples from the great European, colonial sea powers, and he was accepted by them almost immediately. He was applauded by "the German Kaiser, by British believers in empire and admiralty, and then by the American imperialists, led by Roosevelt and Henry Cabot Lodge, [until] by 1913 his ideas had become popular in his own service." (note 6)

The Army, although subject to more varied fortune due to the large-scale mobilization during war and the near collapse during peace, also underwent transformations. Like the Navy, the Army had operated through a series of bureaus, relatively independent of military discipline and of civilian administrative control. The highly independent field commanders and the almost autonomous bureaus were able to manage the post–Civil War frontier fights; but during the Spanish-American War, they had proved eminently inept and wasteful. They could not plan or act in concert in spite of the professionalism of such heirs of Grant as Sherman and Upton. Elihu Root, a corporation lawyer with a great concern for adapting modern business techniques for the public good, was appointed to the War Department in 1899 to bring some order out of the administrative and command confusions. He encountered there some younger officers who had been impressed by the military theories of Clausewitz, which were not unlike those of Mahan in many respects, and by the efficiency of the German Army. As he developed his own notions, which were to become the foundation for reorganization of the services in the twentieth century, Root drew from two major sources: corporation management and the German Imperial Army staff structure. (note 7)

The structure of the bureaus for both the Navy and the Army, as mentioned above, was a series of highly autonomous centers, each going to Congress for its funds and each remaining relatively independent of the others, relatively free from military line or staff control, and from executive coordination. On the executive side, the President had the power of appointment of commanding generals and admirals, usually on an *ad hoc* basis. The notion of a general staff, indeed, was treated as "un-American." In contrast, Root called for the development of a General Staff on the model of the German General Staff, headed by a Chief of Staff who would have immediate direction of the supply bureaus and of the line of command and who would be immediately responsible to the Secretary of War and the President. His intention was to create a clear set of channels for both authority and accountability for the sake of efficient operations, and this required a new professional leadership in the service. (note 8) Many of Root's ideas were adopted in the General Staff Act of 1903.

Root did not succeed in all his notions, however, and was followed by a series of men of limited capacity. But in 1910 Leonard Wood became Chief of Staff and in 1911 Henry Stimson became Secretary of War. They were interested in carrying out the reforms in the field as well as in the military bureaucracy that had begun in the post–Civil War period. The precise character and direction of this program were already manifest in Wood's earlier experience. Wood had commanded the Rough Riders in Cuba and been military governor of the Philippines. He was a close friend of Roosevelt and shared many of his ideas, including those developed by Mahan. And he was working in a structure developed by Root. His immediate major contribution was "to convert the ground forces from a collection of Indian fighters into a modern army." (note 9) But also, "in Cuba and in the pacification of the Philippines, he combined repressive tactics with a benevolent administration to set an American pattern of military government," (note 10) and continually set forth plans to educate the professional military men specifically and the nation at large in the ideals of "national service." (note 11)

Thus, anticipated in the Civil War and the post-bellum developments and given powerful impetus by the experience of becoming a world power in the Spanish-American War, the pattern for military organization was established. Mahan, Root, and Wood were the Plato, Aristotle, and Alexander of American military orientation. Subsequent developments are variations on these three themes: the integration of military power and foreign policy through *Realpolitik* conceptions of international competition defended by the military; integration of industrial supply and military strategy through a professional staff set aside from civilian soldiers, organized by a synthesis of business management techniques and Imperial Army command procedures; and operations in the field through repressive tactics and benevolent policy. It is true that the Navy accented strategic concepts and the Army organizational ones and that this discrepancy led to rather acute inter-service struggles throughout the twentieth century. Nevertheless, the ingredients for unification were already present. The result was a gradually shaping nucleus that has many of the marks of the modern Military-Industrial Complex, and has also allowed the nation to move toward a fourth type of military organization and orientation. The decisive modifications of this general pattern came about through internal development, external threat, and technological innovation.

When the military organizations were called back into public view during World War I, the concepts and structures that had been developed during the preceding half century were given a major test. The "Great War" was won, in part, by the new professionalism of the military and the industrial capacity of the nation. The National Defense Act of 1920 was passed to consolidate the structures that had been developed. And further steps were already in the offing. During the war, several proposals had been made to unify the services and provide them with a single procurement department for the sake of efficiency. There were structural inhibitions to this move. The Navy operated on a model of relatively discreet branches and bureaus loosely associated through a horizontal coordinating procedure. The Army was, according to the German model, more vertically organized. The Republican victory of 1920 brought an administration to office that was concerned for business efficiency. (note 12) The intention was to develop a military "civil service" that would be compatible with the new-found professionalism of the military branches, and which would be freed from both inter-service rivalry and from political pressures and machinations. The proposals failed, due to both Navy and Army opposition, but the failure was temporary. The Navy and the Army over the next twenty years increasingly approximated each other in internal organizational style, and were forced to work together during World War II. Unification and new procedures for unified procurement were finally to come only in the 1950s and 1960s.

From the time of World War I, an additional ingredient was introduced into the mix. The Air Force began as a division of the Signal Corps prior to the war, but separated with rapid enlargement during the war. The role of the Air Force was minimal in winning the war, but its possibilities engendered considerable enthusiasm among professional men who saw its potentiality, air buffs generally, and American industrialists. As Hammond points out:

> Their motivations were bound to be mixed: the aviation program obviously meant more business activity and profits. . . . It represented also a challenge to American industry. Perhaps more significant for the future political appeal of airpower in the United States than either of these, it represented an alternative strategy for winning the war which was much more attractive than trench warfare and more compatible as well with American isolationism and the business-oriented society. The promise of airpower, that is to say, was at once to avoid the mass slaughter of the new mass warfare, to minimize the American commitment abroad, particularly the commitment of American lives and at the same time to give the American business community a more dominating role. . . . (note 13)

This new phenomenon of air power was eventually to create a new and distinct service in rivalry with both the Army and Navy and with peculiar links to the business community.

The internal structures of all services nevertheless developed an internal professionalism on the base erected between the Civil War and World War I. During both the boom of the twenties and the bust of the thirties, when the public eye focused on the American economic condition and the military had to retreat once again into itself, the Navy and the Army, and even the fledgling Air Force, extended the professional character of their organizations. Indeed, all the decisive social marks of a profession begin to appear in full force: a conscious attempt to relate a special body of theory to practice, beyond the level of a general liberal education; a technical competence for which there are standards of excellence, as promotion by seniority gave way to promotion by merit; a dominant ethic of service to a client, in this case the nation, instead of performing services strictly for commercial gain; and the development of guildlike associations which governed internal discipline, controlled "unprofessional" flamboyant behavior by members and tried to prevent exterior encroachment on prerogatives.

These developments, however, were not always smooth. In contrast to the relative independence of other professional groups, the military branches of service were subject to the vicissitudes of public sentiment which politically controlled the purse strings. The celebration of the military during World War I (note 14) was followed by severe criticism of any military establishment by an odd coalition of radicals and smaller businessmen. (note 15) The former argued that the presence of armies caused or contributed to war and the latter charged that the military was a non-productive, exclusively consuming segment of the economy that entailed bigger government. Both wings of the anti-military forces were informed by residues of pre-Spanish-American war sentiment that wanted to deny the international character of American responsibility and evidenced a strong preference for focus on domestic needs and by a resurgence of religious pacifism that was rooted in the liberal, optimistic theology of the period. It was also informed by the efforts of President Wilson to form an international body that would make war obsolete since the world had been made "safe for democracy." Surely, a new world order without wars and

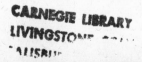
CARNEGIE LIBRARY
LIVINGSTONE ...
"ALISBU"

the instruments of war could be developed around common values and interests.

At the same time, a quiet coalition between the larger corporations and the military was in the making. The connections developed during World War I were cultivated through two decades of inter-war planning between the business community and the armed forces. The War Industries Board, the Office of Assistant Secretary of War and the Business Council were all created during the period and these bodies, with considerable pulling and hauling, developed a series of plans for economic mobilization and industrial-military coordination that actually became the bases of patterns utilized during and after World War II. The men who dominated these boards also dominated the great corporations. (note 16)

When the anti-military orientations were shattered through the new twentieth century fanaticisms of Stalin in Russia and Hitler in Germany, the military and industrial forces came to the fore. In part, these movements demanded a new look at the role of civilian control over military organizations. In part, they evoked the recognition that structural instruments of violence might well be still necessary to contain more vicious instruments of violence. A world without war was unlikely in the face of advocates of violence for the sake of class or race. In part, they manifested new thrusts for economic democracy that were taking place around the world, but they manifested also an incapacity to tolerate the relativism and insecurity deriving from the pluralism that attends democratization. Hence, new economic commonality became limited to mass participation in production and consumption for militant or ecstatic national purposes engineered from above. The total exterior threat demanded the more total mobilization of domestic resources, posed new visions of the results of integration of military, industrial, and ideological power and directly challenged the values that were part of American life. The professional military organizations were hauled out of the wings and on to center stage in World War II and the subsequent Cold War, where they were combined with industrial expansion and mass politics in ways consistent with the theories of Mahan, Root, and Wood.

Both industrial organization and mass politics had undergone transformation during the same period that the military profession was developing. From the burst of rapid corporate expansion during the Industrial Revolution accompanying the Civil War, through the "Robber Baron" era, the trust-busting of the early twentieth century, the free-wheeling euphoria of the twenties, and the hard times of the thirties, industrial life was emerging as a complex pattern in American life, an integral part of the urbanization that was characteristic of the nation.

Three factors were particularly important in the transformation. First, there was the beginning of democratization of the corporation. The new corporations formed during the last third of the nineteenth century almost all followed a single pattern or organization. They were headed by an owner-manager who, with members of his family, directed corporate operations from top to bottom. As the industrial revolution forced the concentration and mechanization of labor, however, and as cities concentrated labor and market resources, larger sizes of corporations became optimal. More capital investment was needed than could be supplied by the resources of one family. The rapid development of public stock ownership was an attempt to broaden the base of capital, resources, and risk. New structures of management were devised requiring the training of personnel from beyond the family. The technological and managerial innovations allowed corporations of great concentration to develop. In this situation, corporate leadership was more and more divorced from ownership. (note 17)

Second, the modest democratization of ownership entailed in this process was accompanied by trust building and by the rise of labor. The trusts threatened to move the industrial system into a new "feudalism" of gigantic proportions. Only the antitrust legislation of the early part of the twentieth century modified this tendency—and that was relatively ineffective until the New Deal period. The rise of labor, as immigrant and rural population moved to the city and began to develop the more complex forms of organization appropriate to the new environment, brought the weakening of single centers of decision-making as trade unions and collective bargaining reinforced the democratization process at a different level. Further, as the unions became stronger, they partially counterbalanced the influence of the captains of industry by introducing social legislation, first in the cities and then nationally through machine politics. (note 18) Both owners and unions, however, were often suspicious of the military, the owners because of the taxes required to support them and because they were "non-productive," labor because branches of the military were used to suppress strikes and because working people are more liable to get drafted.

The depression, however, altered the attitudes of both groups toward government and prepared the way for a further modification during the war. In the face of the collapse of the economy, government sought both to alter the structure of the market by intervention and to develop forms of competition (by more vigorous trust-busting) that would produce socially beneficial results. At the same time, efforts were made to guarantee jobs for the unemployed through governmental projects. New positive links between the instruments of production and the government were established, links which, during the mobilization of the total population to combat totalitarianism abroad, were to be strengthened enormously. Indeed, in the common efforts of World War II, industry, labor, and the government, especially the military, moved into positions of mutual interaction, contracting, personnel transfer, and trust that was unprecedented. The new relationships became law in 1946 when the Employment Act was passed. It stated that it was "the continuing policy and responsibility of the Federal Government . . . to promote maximum employment, production, and purchasing power." Governmental intervention in the economy was established; free-market capitalism was a thing of the past.

The new links could not have been established without new managerial techniques. The Industrial Revolution that produced the assembly line required, with increased size and complexity, new styles of decision-making. A form of dispersed and subdivided decision-making under general supervisory guide-lines was becoming more and more a widespread practice with its own skills. The result was the assembly-line decision process. With specialization of function, parts of decisions are made on narrower and narrower issues. These decisions emerge as entities from the line of decision-making in bargaining, consultation, contracting, respecifying, and in redefining as a whole package.

Nor was this massive new structure of decision-making confined to business, labor, and government contracts. The invasion of Europe by the Allied Forces was itself a monumental feat of coordinated management. The professional military had, within itself, and by borrowing from the structures of the larger society, developed managerial techniques beyond comprehension half a century earlier when they were engendered.

The tentative moves toward economic democratization and toward governmental involvement in and, indeed, control of the market, however, do not exhaust the story. A third factor was decisive—new weaponry. Nowhere was this more striking than in the strides made in aircraft development and production and in atomic energy. Many areas of innovation in research, development, production, and distribution were mothered by the necessity for mobilization and midwifed by new links of the military and the corporation, but none show the overall trends so clearly as the aircraft and the atomic bomb. Air power became the source of a new industry as great corporations sprang into being to fulfill military contracts, utilizing the new systems of large-scale management and assembly-line production and decision-making. Regions of the country previously relatively agrarian and commercial became industrialized and urbanized with unsettling rapidity to fulfill military needs. Atomic energy brought academics into the political-military arena in new and dramatic ways and forecast the new era of economic, industrial, and military resources that were to be a part of the world's future. It is more than symbolic that World War II ended when an airplane dropped an atomic bomb. (note 19)

The implications of these developments are several: in the 1930s and '40s a complex of military and industrial resources, under government sponsorship, had to be mobilized to defeat terrifying unities of government and industry abroad and to end the domestic economic chaos created by the "free market" corporatism. That complex, once mobilized, has in its several parts and in its interrelations developed a professionalized "technostructure" (note 20) committed to the perpetuation of the corporation or military branch in which the manager, the scientist, or the technician finds his identity and a chance to exercise his skills at the forefront of scientific or organizational development. In addition, the nation was at the edge of a new variety of warfare that has turned out to be neither primitive, historic, nor modern. Like primitive warfare, *post–modern* war is fought by the total community in that the masses of population become engaged in the system that produces the new instruments of war. (note 21) This war, too, is fought for the purpose of preserving communal values, and its violence is directed against the great urban centers wherein opposing values are most fully institutionalized. It, too, fulfills cultic obligations and reinforces the social solidarity of the extended group. Like historic war, however, post–modern war tends actually to be fought by professional standing armies armed by weapons makers who are specialists outside the fighting forces. And, like modern war, it is likely to be fought between nations, as justified by international ideology, economics, or politics. Post–modern warfare, however, not only collapses previous distinctions in many regards, it has its own features. It requires a constant source of men, material, organization, and technical innovation never needed before. To plan for a post–modern war, or to plan to defend the nation against a post–modern war, requires a long lead-time and an ever-ready industrial capacity. The further one plans for eventualities of such war in the future and the larger the enterprise planned, the more standing resources are required: aerial delivery systems and atomic weapons cannot be rushed into existence at a moment's notice. To keep these industrial installations not only ready but open at all, relatively constant use of them must be made. But no buyer other than the military can consume their products. In short, segments of the economy must be set aside, structurally linked to the military and governmental bureaucracy and continually nurtured in order to exist.

There was little conscious recognition of this dilemma after World War II. Although the patterns were just below the surface, they were obscured by the pent-up consumer needs of two decades' standing and released by the conclusion of the war. Immediate demobilization and severe curtailing of the military and its links to the economy were the order of the day. The military services, in large measure, were forced again to retreat into their professional shells, as they had after previous wars. The corporations were able to plunge into the booming civilian market. And the public began to recover its historic repugnance to military affairs and its preference for work and the commercial pacifism of the urban shop-keeper. Further, professional politicians began to re-assert more stringent civilian control over the military and its relation to the economy by cutting appropriations, by demanding contract renegotiation in instances of undue profits during the war, and by reorganizing the Department of Defense in the National Security Act of 1947.

The restriction of military influence on national policy and on the economy, however, was not fully successful. It was weakened and ultimately prevented not just by the nature of new forms of warfare and attendant demands for ready industrial and technological resources, but also by a new celebration of American military, industrial, and technological mastery that was clearly part of the national mood. It was prevented as well by the new worldwide responsibilities which had accrued to the most powerful of the victors in the largest of human conflicts and which made its earlier assumption of world power— however hesitant—an undeniable reality. Full restriction was prevented, finally, by the frightened recognition of a former ally and partner in victory as a potential enemy that claimed a manifest destiny contrary to the one claimed by the United States.

The re-identification of Russia and, more broadly, communism as a new national enemy was not slow in coming, although the Soviet Union had been our ally against Germany and Japan. The demands for new forms of community and cooperation needed to dwell in the great, booming cities that had mushroomed out of the pressures of war mobilization brought changes in society, family, and values that threatened many, making them suspicious of social change. To many who were not merely reacting to cosmopolitan social change, Stalin represented the forces of tyranny as much as did Hitler. And the Soviet Union evinced both national and ideological expansionism that had to be contained. Still further, the decisive organizational centers for the new form of war had been suspicious of communism for some time. The professional military had resisted Bolshevism since the twenties, and for thirty years had seen more danger from the Left than from the Right, a view which contributed to its relative unpreparedness during the rise of Hitler. Affinities between the American military organization and that of Germany, ideological appreciation for the role of *Realpolitik*, nationalistic force and violence, and near paranoia in the face of international revolutionary theory or action whether under a red or black flag, made the army more sensitive to communist threats than fascist ones. Businessmen also were violently opposed to nationalization of industry and to any revolutionary shift to state capitalism from corporate capitalism. The religious organizations and spokesmen of the West were antagonistic to godless materialism and critical of the pretentious messianism of the communist ideologies. Unions and voluntary associations, such as the Civil Liberties Union, the NAACP, and the precursors of the ADA, to mention only those most familiar, had fought to maintain control of their organizations against the efforts of communist organizers in the thirties. And the scientific and technological community found the doctrinaire control of research in Russia repugnant to the purposes of their vocations. Politicians saw key values of this society challenged by a new world force. Liberals found Soviet actions in the United Nations as presumptuous about and obstructionist to their visions of a new world order. And when Korea was invaded, all suspicions were confirmed. Anti-communism in its most virulent forms coalesced on the national scene, defining with unreserved vigor a new national enemy and demanding preparations to combat it, to death if necessary. In this context, to work legislatively for federal funding in the area of medicine, poverty, housing, job guarantees, and the whole range of social research was to indicate sympathy for "creeping socialism which leads to communism." Therefore the only way to get certain national priorities looked after was to see that they got listed under national defense. From this period, vast increases in areas of federal funded social activity went to the military, and non-military national priorities began to take on military dimensions.

Few major groups offered qualification to this new and militant crusade that had been brewing since the industrial revolution. The military used the occasion of Korea to reestablish its preparedness and its somewhat attenuated relationship to industry. A new generation of weapons systems had become technologically possible and this was the occasion to reestablish the links which had been in operation during previous conflicts. Samuel Huntington writes on this period, that

> the defense sector became an established [permanent] feature of the American social-economic landscape. Much of the defense production in the Korean War buildup was done by large companies . . . for whom military production was only a small fraction of their total production. After 1953, however, new weapons developments, particularly in aircraft, missiles and electronics, led to the emergence of a large number of companies which were almost completely dependent on the Department of Defense as a purchaser of their products. It was during these years that the industrial segment of the defense sector came into being and that distinct localities began to identify their continued well-being with the presence of defense industry. (note 22)

Established at about 10 percent of the Gross National Product, these defense industries look very much like their civilian counterparts. But they display a distinctive feature. As the new managerial-technological leadership of the non-defense corporations now generated their own capital; as they created, through advertising, new felt needs; as they accepted government action to prevent rapid depression or inflation; and as they planned their own needs by rational calculation of the relative demands of material supply, labor, market, and stock-holders, they achieved a new stability and a programed expansion of the life of the corporations. No longer were the corporations subject to the market; they became increasingly masters of it. The technological-managerial leadership of the defense industries, on the other hand, could not so easily manipulate their market. They were dependent upon a single consumer, and military purchases were subject to the political preferences and policies of the total population as manifest in Congress. To develop the same kinds of self-generating capital and to secure the stability and programed expansion of their corporations, the defense industries had to form at least loose political alliances with military, labor, chamber of commerce, and other groups interested in preventing an uncertain future. They in turn could find support from crusading militarists such as the veterans' organizations. Thus, the situation posed an invitation to "undue" influence. What begins to emerge is a "complex."

The center of the complex is the Department of Defense. Organized by consolidation and coordination of previous institutions under the National Security Act of 1947, this arm of government consists of the Departments of the Army, Navy, and Air Force joined in the Joint Chiefs of Staff under the direction, authority, and control of the Secretary of Defense. It is responsible to the President. It is organizationally linked to the Central Intelligence Agency and the Office of Emergency Planning through the National Security Council.*

---

* As this book goes to press, the "Fitzhugh Report" on reorganization of the Department of Defense has been made public. Its proposals call for reorganizing and lowering in status and authority the Joint Chiefs of Staff, creation of a separate defense staff under a single Chief of Staff, and subordination of the Departments of the Army, Navy, and Air Force. This model of organization was first developed during the late nineteenth century and was a continual minority report in the Mahan, Root, and Wood

The office of Secretary of Defense, which manages and coordinates this vast instrumentality, is actually some four-and-a-half thousand persons making various decisions in either the staff of the Joint Chiefs or in that of the Secretary himself. Key among the latter are: the Director of Defense Research and Engineering, whose primary responsibilities include coordination of research and development with strategy, liaison with research and development groups in the civilian area, and analysis of weapons systems; the Assistant Secretary for Systems Analysis, a relatively new position that has taken over some of the work of analyzing weapons systems with particular attention to the relative costs and effectiveness of various proposals; the Assistant Secretary for Administration, whose assignment is supervision of a host of management tasks from parking-lot assignments to labor effectiveness studies, to internal counter-intelligence, to systematic investigation of long-range management needs; the Comptroller, who prepares the budget estimates and supervises dispersal and bookkeeping; the Assistant Secretary for Installations and Logistics, who is responsible for procuring, transporting, storing, distributing, and disposing of material, and for supervising military buildings and grounds; the Assistant Secretary for International Affairs, who develops and coordinates the Defense Department's position on foreign affairs; the Assistant Secretary for Manpower, who supervises recruitment, training allocation, and support (health, education, benefits, and welfare) of military personnel; the Assistant Secretary for Public Affairs, the public relations officer, who not only deals with news releases, but helps plan testimony before Congress and speeches for major Department officials; and the

---

schools of thought. It became dominant in the organization of the German High Command of World War II. Similar proposals were defeated in Congress during and after World War I and in a series of efforts in the same direction immediately after World War II. Defense Secretary Melvin Laird has apparently forbidden the Joint Chiefs of Staff from either undertaking alternative studies or testifying against the present proposal in Congressional hearings. In net effect, the proposal would "debureaucratize" the highest levels of military command and concentrate military power in the hands of the Chief of Staff. That figure could make more decisions without having to negotiate with competing authorities.

General Counsel who supervises the legal dimensions of contracting, legislation, and criminal or civil cases that pertain to
the Department. In addition there is the extensive staff of the
Joint Chiefs, and a series of defense agencies concerned with
specialized tasks such as developing and testing nuclear weapons (Defense Atomic Support Agency), auditing the procurement, contracting, and distribution of funds (Defense Contract
Audit Agency), and so forth.

The size and complexity of this organization stagger
the imagination. This vast bureaucracy administers a network of
real property and equipment approximately twice the combined
worth of the nation's 100 largest manufacturing corporations.
(note 23)

The budget of the Department of Defense is the largest
single item in our federal budget. Contrary to popular opinion,
however, it is not growing by leaps and bounds (see Table 1).
It has remained and probably will remain relatively stable in
the two decades following the Korean War if measured in terms
of gross national product and percent of federal budget.

If one looks at dollar amounts, one finds the gross national product, the federal budget, the budget of the Department of Defense, and spending on non-defense programs all
going up, even if one controls for inflation. But the rates and
amounts of increase are lowest in the military budget. In recent
years, spending on non-defense programs has begun to approximate defense spending, compromising the notion that the
Military-Industrial Complex is totalistic in its influence. Further,
if one sets aside the bulges in defense spending caused by
Korean and Vietnamese conflicts, it becomes clear that we are
dealing with relatively stable amounts. The problem, of course,
is that the amount is enormous to begin with and that we are
dealing with a well-established social phenomenon which can
generate its own needs.

It is more difficult to grasp the industrial side of the
Complex. Nearly every national industry has the military as a
consumer. From shoe strings and floral arrangements for graves
and monuments to large-scale missile systems and aircraft
carriers, some segment of every market goes to the military.

Fiscal Year	Amount in Millions	Percent of Federal Budget	Percent of Gross National Product
1953	50,442	68.1	14.1
1954	46,986	69.6	13.0
1955	40,695	63.2	10.7
1956	40,723	61.5	10.0
1957	43,368	62.9	10.1
1958	44,234	62.0	10.0
1959	46,491	57.9	9.9
1960	45,691	57.7	9.3
1961	47,494	58.3	9.4
1962	51,103	58.2	9.4
1963	52,755	56.9	9.2
1964	54,181	55.5	8.9
1965	50,163	52.0	7.8
1966	57,652	53.9	8.1
1967	72,183	55.2	8.9
1968	79,899	56.8	9.5
1969*	80,500	57.5	10.0
1970*	80,500	57.5	10.0
1971*	78,500	55.0	9.0
1972*	78,000	54.0	8.5

Table 1: The Defense Budget and the GNP.

(These figures to 1966 are taken from the *Congressional Record*, Nov. 21, 1966. Figures for the years asterisked are my calculations based in part on Charles Schultz, "The Pentagon Shopping List," *The Progressive* (June, 1969), pp. 41 ff.; Samuel Huntington, "The Defense Establishment: Vested Interests and the Public Interest," *The Military-Industrial Complex and U.S. Foreign Policy*, edited by Omer L. Carey (Pullman, Wash.: Washington State University Press, 1969), pp. 1–14; and Edward Brooke, "Billions for Defense, but Not One Cent for Waste," paper delivered at the General Synod of the United Church of Christ, June, 1969).

And 5.2 percent of all civilian employees work in defense industries in addition to the full time civilian employees of the Department of Defense. Ninety percent of national goods and services are consumed by the private sector of the economy, and 90 percent of the working population do not directly or indirectly depend on the Department of Defense. Nevertheless, certain key segments of the economy are decisively dependent upon government contracts and serve as the nucleus of the industrial side of the Complex. Approximately twenty-six billion of the seventy-nine to eighty billion dollars expended by the Department of Defense yearly are or will be localized in some 100 corporations and their subsidiaries for defense hardware. (note 24) And although, year by year, varying amounts are awarded to various corporations, the relative ranking of the major corporations remains relatively stable. Further, these corporations are, as often as not, governed by interlocking directorates. Persons owning large amounts of stock in one of these corporations are likely to hold it in several. (note 25) More decisive, however, is the actual managerial level where personnel are interchangeable. Competition for top executive leadership facilitates considerable job-hopping between similar corporations, providing an informal but real set of links between the structurally diverse corporations on the industrial side of the Complex.

Not only is there interconnection between corporations, but the Department of Defense also has a series of interior and exterior links with the defense corporations that bridge the traditional division of public and private sectors of the political economy and must be seen as part of the total picture. A series of communication and contracting networks joins the corporations to the Department.

The most obvious interior link is that of personnel. Not only do retired generals often possess the managerial skills and technical knowledge that make them useful employees of the corporations, but they maintain personal friendships as well as social and business contacts with men remaining in the Department of Defense. In the other direction, corporation executives, lawyers, and research personnel make the most qualified body of persons from which to draw civilian appointees to the Department of Defense. Further, there are programs whereby aspiring but relatively unwealthy young technological researchers and managerial bureaucrats have their advanced training paid for by the services in return for promises to work in the Department for so many years. These men are often drawn from corporations engaged in DOD research and return to them upon completion of their obligations. Informing this common pool of personnel both editorially and technically are a number of trade and service journals, the pages of which are filled with the interlocking developments in the Department and in the corporations. At another level, the massive work force which is utilized and frequently trained by the DOD is the same work force which, having fulfilled its obligations to the service, is most adept at performing the skills needed by the production-oriented defense corporations. Sometimes veterans are given preference in hiring.

The legal bonds between the corporations and the Department of Defense are extremely complex. Extended procedures and devices for contracting and sub-contracting, for leasing of government facilities by private corporations and providing capital equipment, and for expansion, modification or reduction of contract agreements and profit margin, and for redesigning the specifications in the midst of an assignment have been developed over the past several decades. They present a maze of overlapping directives, clearance requirements, and points of initiation frequently supervised in the corporations by "live-in" representatives of the Department of Defense. The unpredictability of research and development in new areas of technology has made such procedures necessary, and has resulted in more intense communication and consultation than is necessary in civilian contracting. Further, many of the products of the corporation are so designed that there can only be one consumer. No one else besides the government buys weapons or guidance systems of the same magnitude. The result, on the one hand, is a jungle of managerial-legal relationships that teems with new technological undergrowth and sustains fertile ideas within its own confines. On the other hand, this jungle becomes increasingly impenetrable to the outsider and becomes so concentrated on the maintenance of its rather unique life, as Galbraith properly contends, that it tends to become constitutionally separated from the surrounding forms of existence. Its legal basis of operation and its governing rules are at present pertinent only in the context of Department of Defense contracting. (note 26)

There are also exterior links to the Department. The president who appoints the chief administrative personnel for the Department of Defense and the Congress that votes funds for it also have constituencies. The level of employment, the general regional economic welfare, and the specific life or death of major corporations depend upon the contractual relationships awarded to the industries by the Department of Defense. Any major reduction in funds would mean serious economic dislocation likely also to have political repercussions. More personal factors have implications as well: no political candidate finds it detrimental to have proven military experience and corporation backing. Many a congressman has earned or been awarded honorary military rank and close contact with the corporations who wish to use his political influence to assist in securing or keeping military installations or contracts. The campaign slogan of Mendel Rivers, the late chairman of the House Armed Services Committee, "Rivers Delivers," is only one of the most blatant examples of this indirect set of links between the Pentagon and the chambers of commerce back home.

Also in the political arena, many major corporations have international holdings and deal constantly with the Department of State in working out sticky relations or the protection of property in foreign lands. The military, also, has its own influence in the Department of State, in spite of rivalry, and is deeply concerned about preserving American interests abroad. Indeed, there are links from almost every department of government to almost every other. Even the Office of Economic Opportunity, one of the most progressive instrumentalities for domestic welfare, sometimes works with the defense corporations and with the DOD in job training and placement. (note 27)

Of greater concern, recently, has been the influence of the Department and the defense companies in the universities and in academic societies. Indeed, the link is so significant that several observers claim that one must speak of a "Military-Industrial-Academic Complex." The centers of scientific-technological ideas and basic research are the universities and non-profit institutions often clustered around them, and the academic societies that bring together leading minds in physics, biology, chemistry, various phases of engineering, indeed, the whole range of pure and applied sciences, as primary forums wherein new ideas, theories, and insights are brought before a community of peers. This level of scientific and technological research is fundamental to all other levels and stands as the root from which all future weapons systems, managerial techniques, control systems, and communication systems will derive. The universities and non-profit institutions not only have direct grants from the Department of Defense, totaling some 10 percent of the amount spent for all research and development, but many individual professors and researchers in the university are also related to independent non-profit corporations engaged in defense research. These corporations, in turn, subcontract work from profit corporations. More directly, leaders in the major defense corporations may sit on the boards of trustees or overseers of the major universities. The majority of the funding, guidance, and concerns of the university may remain outside this set of links, but the links are present and strong nevertheless, and deeply disturbing to many scientists and technologists whose primary concern is carrying out research for purposes of increasing knowledge, but who find that the only adequate and available source of funds is the military. (note 28)

Further, scientists and technologists complain privately about the impossibility of attending academic conferences and presenting papers without being deluged by representatives of DOD's "inhouse labs" or the defense corporations pressing questions about the particular applicability of the research to national security or without hearing papers from these men which do have or are expected to have military pay-off value. Indeed, these forums not only promote idea exchange, but they have also become hiring exchanges for personnel with promising notions.

The difficulty of pursuing "pure" research is that no scientific research is value-free, at one point, at least. Some value judgment has to be made as to what is most important to do, what questions need to be asked, and what areas need to be researched. The Department of Defense, which is the source of funds for much of the research, and the corporations who are primarily concerned with developing ideas that can be worked into a proposal, form two strong sides of a triangle that greatly influence the direction of science and technology. Further, one key center for this academic link is found in the "think tank." RAND, RAC, and SORO (the Air Force, Army, and Navy research corporations) are highly significant centers wherein the hard technological possibilities are researched in relation to the "soft sciences," politics, economics, social organization, etc. It is these organizations, populated by experts from nearly every field, that constitute a non-teaching, military "university"; an idea-proving ground to test out ideas generated elsewhere and to generate its own concepts of structure, technology, policy, and their interaction.

There are indications that this triangle has become counter-productive in some degree. At many of the major institutions such as M.I.T., Southern California, and Johns Hopkins, as well as many other universities with less involvement, minorities deeply suspicious of this set of links are demanding reassessment of them. Further, as the 1969 summer debate on the ABM showed, numerous scientific and technological experts with political sensitivities contrary to the DOD and the defense corporations made public their well-informed judgments in opposition to those interests. But the influential set of indirect links shows few signs of weakening nevertheless.

The term *Military-Industrial Complex*, then, does have a specific meaning, even if it can only be outlined in a study of this sort. It is made of specific institutions and specifiable links between them. It is not simply a bunch of dishonest businessmen and generals conspiring to feather their own nests or run the economy. It is not simply blood-thirsty merchants of death. It is not the whole of American society, however massive it may appear. Nor is it the simple product of recent political economics and a technostructure.

The Complex is more widespread than a few bad eggs in the corporations or the Pentagon, although they can indeed be found. It is more subtle than creeping militarism engineered by contemporary successors to the war profiteers and imperialists. Were these its roots, there is little evidence that we could make generals and businessmen more honest or that we could convert militarists to a new world view. The secular preachers who see, as we noted in chapter 2, the problem of the Military-Industrial Complex as a systemic problem related to the historic values of the society and to the political-economic structures of the nation are more accurate. Yet it is neither the whole of the American character, nor the specific structure of the Pentagon brass, of partisan political parties, or of the corporations that can easily be identified as the culprit. The Military-Industrial Complex is a diversified cluster of institutions bound together by common values and history and sustained by a multiplicity of internal and external linkages.

This definition is not yet satisfying, however, for this new social grouping is not a comfortable monolith. It is clearly not a class phenomenon in traditional terms. The managerial-technological groups are at its heart, but its needs, are so great that large-scale training, scholarship offerings, and continual possibilities for mobility appear to bring about opportunities *relatively* open to persons from a number of social-economic backgrounds. It is also not an easy monolith in terms of ordinary political ideology. Representatives of romantic, localist, universalist, and reactionary postures populate the complex. Indeed, in spite of efforts to control such things, leaks on all sides of the debates on ABM, MIRV, and Viet Nam feed investigators looking for ammunition on different sides of the aisle and on opposite sides of the question. Nor is it totally integrated structurally. It contains highly competitive sub-groups working at swords' points. Not only are there strong residues of the inter-service rivalry between Army, Navy, and Air Force, and the sometimes vicious competition for contracts between the corporations, but in the branches of service and in the corporations factions continue to struggle for a larger cut of the pie and more say in the kinds of contracts that are to be proposed, awarded, or taken. The vision of a militaristic monolith is no more accurate than the nineteenth century Protestant's view of Catholicism or the red-baiter's view of the international communist conspiracy. But there are in the Military-Industrial Complex, impersonal sets of formal and informal governing roles, rules, and relations, through which the real differentiation occurs.

The structures that can be identified and specified represent only ten percent of our population and economy, less than that of our academic life, and probably no more than that of the issues that preoccupy those organizations that have taken on responsibility for the moral and political welfare of the nation— the churches, the voluntary associations, and political and social pundits. The problem is that this ten percent is structurally linked with approximately half of our official federal organization. And the structural links are so efficient, so complex, and so rich in resources and possibilities in spite of internal competition, gross blunders, and stultifying red tape, compared to other organizations of the same scale, that a new social phenomenon is established of very significant proportions. Never, in the history of man, has any single set of institutions of comparable size been so well organized. It has taken on a life of its own with its own internal logic and culture. It predisposes its members to see all problems, foreign and domestic, as malleable to a technological, managerial, contractual, research solution. Persons who do not fit this pattern of interacting roles are shunted aside and moved out of the informal matrix of personal relations that sustain the formal system. That system generates its own definition of needs and mobilizes its own resources to meet those needs. If one must identify a single image to capture the nature of this phenomenon, it cannot be corrupt generals or businessmen, "merchants of death," "power elite," the whole of society, or the technostructure of corporations. If anything, the Military-Industrial Complex can only be compared in richness and complexity to a modern metropolis. Indeed, it is in some ways more complex and post-urban; for it is freed from any specific geographical boundary and it has greater techno-logical-managerial capacity than any contemporary metropolis. Looked at socio-historically, then, the Military-Industrial Complex can be defined as a specific set of impersonal, interlocking institutional structures, rooted in the history of urban industrial society and in the specific conflicts of America's emergence as a world power. It is governed by generalized value patterns that transcend ordinary political ideology; it is undergirded by a matrix of personal, contractual, and fiscal linkages, and it is centered in the relationships of the Department of Defense to major corporations. These social mechanisms and structures set the pace for post-urban society.

CHAPTER FOUR

The core of the complex: its values

We have seen, so far, that the strictly political and economic definitions of the Complex are inadequate and that they need to be supplemented by a social-historical analysis to expose how deeply rooted the phenomenon is in our social history. Expectations of immediate solutions by exposing militaristic skulduggery by demonstrations, by electing liberals to public office, or economic conversion can only be a preface to social and political disillusionment—as is indeed occurring among many of the disciples and devotees of the secular preachers treated in chapter 2. We have also seen that the phenomenon of the Military-Industrial Complex did not leap forth out of the peculiar conditions of the Cold War, but is rooted in deeper and broader social movements of the past century from which the Cold War itself partly derived.

But neither a cross-sectional analysis, one that tries to look at the Complex as it stands, nor a longitudinal analysis, one that tries to see the historical development of the Complex, nor these in combination yet render a sufficient interpretation of a major social phenomenon. The Complex does not maintain its status, nor did it develop over a century, by overt coercive means. And no institution or matrix of institutions is caused by inevitable social forces alone. Social pressures bring about the occasion for institutions to arise, decline, retrench, redesign, or reorganize, but they do not completely determine which occurs and in what direction. In the midst of social pressures, people *argue* that such and such changes *ought* or *ought not* to be made. Such arguments are based on the internal *raison d'être* of an organization or complex of organizations which have a unique set of drives, goals, and purposes; and they are based on appeals to overarching cultural presuppositions as to what is

right and *good* and *fitting* to do. The organizational and ideological concerns of Mahan, Root, and Wood have been brought
into dominance by a whole set of external and internal influences which also modified their original character. The wide-
ranging group of sources which have been identified as social
in the previous chapter are supplemented by another broad set
of influences that can be called "values," an ingredient that is
recognized but not systematically treated by Hayden, Kolko,
Galbraith, and Barnet.

In the development of the Military-Industrial Complex
during the past century, there were critical moments when the
military and industrial institutions could have developed in different directions. There is, however, a significant degree of
continuity throughout its development in spite of the fact that
specific social, political, economic, and technological influences
shifted, and in spite of the enormous turnover in personnel at
all levels. That fact indicates that larger cultural pressures, generalized senses of what ought to be done that change much
slower than specific social forces, played some role in shaping
these institutions. They were not developed by sheer force. The
developments took place for the most part by consent of those
affected. In arguing for or against specific developments in
Congress, or in the office of the Secretary of Defense, in campaign promises, in public forums, spokesmen appealed to com-
monly held goals to win the point. When people pour their lives
into professional military service, defense corporations, or research on defense contracts, they seek or find purposes in such
activity that transcend the pay check. They do not act as passive
victims of social history. And when certain kinds of evidence are
cited as legitimizing specific policy, they make value-laden assumptions about how one should interpret human nature, the
trends of history, and the relative worth of various social perspectives. These goals, purposes, and assumptions are affirmed
or confessed "values" that determine the responses of men and
institutions to specific social pressures as much as the pressures
themselves. People may not consciously choose the consequences of these values, but cumulative choices on the basis of
chosen values have consequences. And while it is argued by

some that the values are themselves a product of the social forces, one can just as well argue that the social forces are themselves shaped by previously held values. Values and social forces interact so subtly and in such a complex manner that to ignore one in favor of the other is reductionistic.

Further, a social phenomenon as vast and as complicated as the Military-Industrial Complex takes on an intrinsic set of values which become organized in an enduring system. People come and go; policies are made, abandoned, and remade; organizational charts are revised weekly; negotiations on contracts are carried on by a succession of personnel representing multiple parties, and yet a whole set of assumptions, purposes and goals remains relatively stable. The machinations of persons, as often treated by political science, the forming of specific *ad hoc* alliances as reported in liberal and conservative journals, and continual new accents in newspapers about military-industrial matters all seem, and are, highly idiosyncratic unless one can see some larger patterns. And there are such patterns. Like any major social institution, the Military-Industrial Complex has an inner logic. A way of looking at life becomes embodied in that Complex. It becomes embodied in various procedures, policy directives, kinds of persons promoted or seeking promotion, ranking of first and second priorities and a thousand similar facets of normal operating procedure. People outside may hold similar views; people or even departments inside may hold contrary views; and a wide spectrum of disagreement may be held among those involved. But the Complex itself tends to be organized around, to claim its legitimacy by, and to demand some degree of loyalty from its members to the inner logic of values at its core. For some the matter is simply one of having a regular job and pay check; but others have deeper motivations. "Men serve these organizations in many, if not most instances," writes John Kenneth Galbraith, "because they believe in what they are doing—because they have committed themselves to the bureaucratic truth." (note 1) This core, this institutional "soul," is a fundamental ingredient. Contrary to the views that weaponry has produced policy and values or that policy has produced weaponry and institutions, it is here suggested that institutionalized values are independent factors in the production of weaponry and policy. And it is further suggested that values outside and within the institutions determine in large measure the nature and structure of the institutions and their responses to social forces.

Thus, if we are to proceed further in the analysis of the Military-Industrial Complex, we must identify those goals, purposes, and assumptions that have been at least as influential as social history has been. Indeed, one must engage in a "value" analysis on at least two levels: the overarching values that have affected the social history producing the Complex and the inner values of the Complex itself.

The Military-Industrial Complex developed during the period when this country moved from an agrarian to an urban society and became international in its perspective. We must start there. Other large countries in the new world did not make that transition. Enormous numbers of people moved from agrarian backgrounds to metropolitan areas and world travel by joining the Army to get out of where they were or by getting a job in industry to get a part of the new world. Rural patterns of family, economy, and politics, localistic patterns of loyalty and monolithic styles of life were abandoned in favor of greater individual freedom, wider horizons, and loyalty to larger goods. Some went through the universities where the deprovincialization process was more self-conscious and rationalized. For others, exposure to a pluralism of social and cultural style, and direct participation in an institution serving the whole nation deprovincialized attitudes and provided an occasion for new fragments of cosmopolitan values to become a part of the horizon of larger and larger percentages of the population. The cosmopolitan values were not long confined to the cities. Through communication, through mobility, through education, and through economic or political powers located in the cities, the urban values spilled over the countryside, and the goals, purposes, and assumptions previously most manifest in the cities —an *urban* ethos—became part of *national* culture.

In the urban ethos, people and institutions depended upon mastery of their environment. Artifacts, not nature, became the dwelling place of man, dependent upon and resulting in the extension of planning and technological transformation.

Planning requires a particular perspective, a distinctive set of values. It demands a notion of history that sees man and his environment as malleable to human control. It allows calculation of probability and possibility and the taking of steps to meet eventualities. It invites living in the future, for man is free to do so. Man has not always lived thus. The overwhelming number of centuries of human history give evidence of living in bondage to the past, of presupposing that the inherited structures will be and should be valid in the future. But under the impact of the Judeo-Christian tradition, particularly as it was developed in the Calvinist revolution, specific aspects of the tradition—those breaking organic ties to dimensions of the past, those accenting transformation, and those subduing traditionalistic forces in favor of a new social order—moved into dominance and spurred the reorganization of man's conception of his future. The future is open to organized redefinition precisely because man is free to build a new commonwealth. (note 2)

Further, man is free to utilize the forces of nature against nature. He may engage in technological transformation to achieve human ends for the glory of that power which gave man freedom. (note 3) That is, he may do as he will because he can.

It is these views which developed the urban ethos when linked with other factors in the environment such as a monied economy, which freed man from bondage to geographical plots of ground; technological capability, which allowed actual and not just theoretical transcendence over nature; and population density, which required some kind of reorganization. And it is in the context of these goals and capabilities that the Military-Industrial Complex grew.

But the Military-Industrial Complex appropriated these values and is a product of them in specific ways. It is a subculture that understands these purposes in a distinct fashion. Professional military personnel do not come from urban backgrounds, but from agrarian and small town backgrounds in overwhelming percentages, as Janowitz has shown. (note 4) But professional soldiers became aware of and concerned with some aspects of the urban ethos because of technological change. Living in the future through planning is seen in the context of the primary professional value of providing "security." The first responsibility of military organizations is to discern external threats to the freedom of the nation and to plan for all eventualities relevant to that threat. Consequently, the military organizations must use every technological device available to meet challenges, to counteract technology of potential enemies, and to extend the range of control over further areas so that planning can be done. It is not a constructive responsibility, but a defensive responsibility. (note 5) Hence the military planner "must be conservative in his calculations; that is, he must prepare for the worst plausible case and not be content to hope and prepare merely for the most probable." (note 6)

The urbanization of the American ethos not only involved values pertinent to planning and technology, it involved a new definition of order. Urbanization requires a plurality of subdivisions and styles of life, but they must be integrated at certain points through voluntary agreement to impersonal routines. A more monolithic structure appropriate to a feudal society or a practical communitarianism of the village or small town cannot be sustained. Too much division of labor, too much specialization of function, too many people to bear the psychic weight of total involvement of each with each, prevails for the common order of previous societies to be effective. (note 7) Order is not imposed from without so much as attained from within by voluntary compliance to an internalized collective consciousness on the part of free persons and free institutions. Such order derives from a sense of duty and tolerance—the duty of each man to fulfill his obligation in the total order for the sake of the commonwealth, and tolerance for persons whose life styles and arenas of operations are decidedly different. This has produced a highly individualistic culture that expects each man to pay his own way and guarantees him the right to do so by protection of private property. The commonwealth, thus, is not so much a common structure of wealth as it is the conglomerate wealth of many individuals. Further, each individual is to allow maximum freedom to his neighbor in the name of tolerance. In the *laissez-faire* days of modern industrial society, these motifs were articulated through the language of Protestant piety and social Darwinism in terms of rights of private contract (which allowed a powerful corporation to negotiate wages with a powerless worker), in terms of the providential character of competition to assure survival of the fittest (which turned out to mean survival of the most vicious), and in terms of systematic denial of the rights of the government or the workers to organize in such a way that they could interfere with these distorted senses of duty and tolerance (which prevented early passage of social legislation). In later phases of urbanized industrial development, however, the rights of the labor force to organize and of the government to "interfere" in limited ways for the sake of the commonwealth were recognized. At the same time, managerial and educational techniques were developed which allowed individual persons liberty in wider and wider ranges of specialization and decision-making over narrower and narrower ranges of issues. And duty became defined as the capacity to master a specific area. Instead of responsibility for the overall shape of the commonwealth, the ethics of duty became the ethics of achievement in one's specialty. Further, tolerance was specified as allowing a pluralism of centers of loyalty to exist—centers religious, ethical, political, economic, and professional—as power concentrations which often engaged in shifting coalitions on particular issues. (note 8) The result was a lack of clear accountability for the general shape of things.

The Military-Industrial Complex has adopted and adapted these motifs in specific ways. The definition of order which it is to defend, and indeed, extend, is one of individualistic capitalism. Order is not to be imposed from without, but by voluntary agreement. Hence, the Complex has long been deeply hostile to non-individualistic or non-capitalist totalitarian countries. It has deeply rooted moral preferences for a volunteer army which sees its duty in times of national crisis and voluntarily relinquishes ordinary citizen rights to assume the discipline required for national defense. Indeed, full-time professionals give their lives voluntarily to rather rigid, highly struc-

tured, impersonal, routinized activities under a sense of duty
and order for the commonwealth. Yet the Complex manifests
tolerance, also—great tolerance for personal idiosyncrasies in
ideology, private life, and, to a degree, in official life; but military personnel are restrained by code and conscience from being too vocal on the overall shape of American political life not
specifically in their area of competence. Furthermore, the existence of a multiplicity of free corporations bound only by freely
negotiated contracts to the military is deemed superior to direct
government ownership or management.

In order to plan and to exercise technological skills,
however, and to fulfill and extend duty and tolerance in the
name of that "order we call liberty," it has become necessary to
more closely integrate and coordinate the instruments that guarantee them. Thus, the Military-Industrial Complex has become
one of the most socialistic systems in the world. Birth-to-death
care, state ownership of the tools of employment, and central-
ized planning are clearly established. The Protestant-engen-
dered urban goals of freedom to plan and transform nature, as
modified under the impact of concern for security, and the goal
of order as redefined by shifting meanings of duty and tolerance, have taken up residence in a socialized subculture which
controls 10 percent of the nation's economy—a subculture more
intensively integrated than any other segment of the society.

These goals are reinforced by the more immediate purposes of men. Military personnel and industrial personnel in the
defense sector have a genuine sense of personal vocation, at
least as deep as other institutions in society. Although professional military and defense industrial personnel do not suffer
from noticeable deprivation, they often do not get the economic
rewards or the social esteem that could be gained outside. They
are often motivated, instead, by a commitment to the service of
the country and to mankind. (note 9) Not only may soldiers
be called upon to sacrifice their lives for the nation in death,
but they pour out their lives, while living, to prepare themselves, others and the material wherewithal for the defense and
security of the society. Just as the dominant urban-industrial
ethos has been created by and in turn required an extensive

ethic of proficiency and service to the population on the part of politicians, sanitation engineers, repairmen, retail establishments, consumer industries and so on ad infinitum, so those engaged in the Military-Industrial Complex see their roles in terms of proficiency and service. If they are military managers, they are not only developing the newest kinds of large-scale organizational techniques for one of the largest interlocking sets of institutions in the history of man, they also are serving for the sake of the whole commonwealth. (note 10) If they are researchers or developers they are not only working at the forefront of scientific or technological research to conquer nature and extend man's control of his environment, but they are doing it for the sake of the country. The personal and professional values of urbanized, industrial society are integrated and coordinated for the service of the nation.

There is, undoubtedly, coincidence of interest in these phenomena, and much rationalization of values. Adam Yarmolinsky has recently written on this point with characteristic realism:

> The interest of the defense industry in maintaining a constant (or expanding) level of procurement coincides with the interest of military officers in developing new weapons systems for which they have been assigned program responsibility. It coincides also with the interest of labor union leaders in keeping their members on the job; with the interest of individual Congressmen in maintaining full employment and prosperity in their Congressional districts; and with the interests of lawyers, bankers, public relations men, trade association executives and journalists and a host of others whose professional and personal fortunes depend on this major sector of the U. S. economy. [But] the coincidence of these interests does not suggest any nefarious combination or conspiracy among the various elements of the military establishment. *The overwhelming majority is motivated by a genuine concern for national security* [italics mine]. (note 11)

In short, at the level of motivation of men choosing the Military-Industrial Complex as the locus for their personal vocations, there is a peculiar adaptation of the goals of urban-technological society to a set of institutionalized roles given sanction in terms of service to national purpose. The particular and various purposes of men in these institutionalized roles reinforce goals and find legitimation in the values of national security and defense.

The subcultural goals and the more personal purposes are given further support by fundamental value ingredient-assumptions of another sort. At the core of the Military-Industrial Complex, and in the private philosophy of large numbers of its personnel, lies a social-historical Philosophy of Man.

Man is a social animal; but he is a contentious social animal, forever engaging in conflict. The social world consists in competing forces that continually threaten to get out of control. Civilization as we know it is fragile and besieged by forces within and without that must be checked. The constant lesson of history is that men and societies must continually devise new techniques to bring about control of the destructive forces. And while reason is itself continually subject to man's irrational passions, it is reason alone that can provide the kinds of ordered discipline that can prevent chaos. The mind of the Military-Industrial Complex, thus, is conservative. But it is not necessarily conservative in the sense of *laissez-faire* economics. It is conservative in its overriding concern to preserve civilizational values as they actually are and in its pessimistic, realistic recognition of the need for disciplined authority and hard calculation. Its contempt for idealistic liberalism that thinks it can save the world by permissiveness is widespread. (note 12)

On the military side of the Complex, this motif manifests itself in the hard-headed "calculus of risk" in the strategy of international affairs. (note 13) On the technological research and industrial side, it becomes manifest in the rigors of the drive for quantification through systems analysis and the hard sciences. And in the administrative side, it shows up in the cost-benefit tough-mindedness made familiar under the leadership of Robert McNamara. (note 14)

Disciplined authority and hard calculation are necessary, under this philosophy, because history is a perennial cycle of war and peace and war and peace. The natural state of man is war, and he inevitably settles his disputes through violence. Peace is a temporary stalemate brought on when contenders rationally recognize the impossibility of victory, or, if they are governed by irrationality, have a failure of will. This is a "natural law of man and history." While nature itself can be transformed, neither human nature, with man's contentious semi-rationality, nor history, with its clashing societies, can be altered. Man can only work within the confines of these "facts," and rationally try to plan for them. Thus, to operate within the laws of man and history, it becomes necessary to gain a superior force by transforming nature technologically. A clearly superior force may either rationally convince, or irrationally frighten, a potential enemy into restraint. If it does neither, the security and defense of the system is assured, for the wherewithal is available to resist attack. Technology then becomes, on the one hand, something of a moral substitute for war and, on the other hand, a guarantee of victory or survival should the substitute fail. If war does not come, it will be because of the technical preparedness of the military, although the preparations would then *appear* to have been unnecessary. If war does come, it will be because of lack of preparedness, although then it will seem to have been obviously necessary.

People engage in the technology race with a this-worldly asceticism and zeal that is comparable only to religious motivation. For quasi-religious values and commitments are held with regard to the basic assumptions. Questions of ultimate power and questions of final worth are at stake in this peculiar form of somewhat fatalistic civil religion. Men give time, energy, dedication, and hard work, and continually request more financial resources to secure, according to the natural law of history, both the survival of the nation and the continued quality of life that it represents, especially political democracy and economic affluence. Commitment at the highest level is both for the *esse* and *bene esse* of existence. And if these are allowed to continue by our firmness of adherence to them and our rational preparation for their defense, it is presupposed that allegiance to these values has providentially proven correct.

What the Military-Industrial Complex is for, at the highest cultural level of a national quasi-theology, is supplemented by what it is against. The Military-Industrial Complex has come into full bloom in response to communism. Communism is viewed in terms of a counter-force with a counter-history and legitimized by counter-values. At every level, communism is viewed as the contrary of what this society stands for. It is in this century the force of evil that must be defended against. Where the urban goal of pluralism is valued, it is understood as confronted by a monolith. The Western mastery of environment for the sake of man's freedom is counterposed by the Eastern control of men for the sake of the ideal environment of a grand, new society. Planning, in order to live in the future, is seen under communism to become tyrannical coordination in order to bring about an apocalypse. Order by voluntary compliance and multiple-centered management is understood by the Military-Industrial Complex to be transformed into unified dictatorship under communism. Relative degrees of economic democracy that obtain under communism are not noticed or deemed valuable. Commitment to duty and achievement and personal vocation through rational discipline in the West is contrasted with fanaticism in the East. And the assumptions about the providential control of destructive forces that would create chaos are made in the face of the very source of that destruction and chaos.

Communism is not viewed as a vision of social and economic democracy that is itself pluralistic and cosmopolitan in several respects; it is a counter-culture, a counter-civilization and a counter military-industrial complex that must be contained, deterred, or defeated.

The quasi-theological assumptions of the Military-Industrial Complex are not universally held in so simple a form by all within the fold. The Complex contains "denominations" and "sects" that have intense doctrinal disagreements. The defense industries sometimes diverge from the military establishment. The Army and the Navy and the Air Force compete on ideological as well as strategic and political grounds on many occasions. But the most decisive doctrinal debates are carried on between the "militants" and the "moderates" that often cross cut the organizational lines. If, for example, we compare the writings of Melvin Laird to the writings of Robert McNamara, we can see divergent interpretations of major motifs pointed to above. (note 15) These two most recent Secretaries of Defense are in many ways distinct ideological heirs of Mahan, Root, and Wood as modified by the development of managerial and technological urban patterns of values and by the rise of communism.

Melvin Laird, in his book written while chairman of the House Defense Appropriations Subcommittee, (note 16) begins with a call to dialogue, and an assertion that the whole question to be discussed is the question of "life's meaning." (note 17) Strategy is dependent upon objectives, objectives on priorities, priorities on values, and values on "an attitude on life itself." (note 18) That is what is finally decisive in military organization.

Laird's attitudes are rather clear. He is arguing against those who see only a mushroom cloud hanging over the cities of man. (note 19) In contrast, he draws upon Erik Voegelin, author of *The World of the Polis*, to ground his view of national priorities for preservation of modern industrial urban society on eternal truths that must be conserved at the risk of death. The need for strategy and for large-scale military and industrial preparedness to defend these truths comes from the threat of disorder, through which communism advances by force. (note 20) To counteract that, a reassertion of "right order" is required, a reassertion of "right order" based on real, everlasting truth presaged in the American Revolution.

> "It was a revolution of men committed not to their personal passions or to half-understood abstractions, but to order, to belief in a God beyond history and above government. . . . They appealed to a whole system of es-

tablished ethics, to Him they called as Supreme Judge of the World. . . . These values, these commitments beyond the physical or merely material, did not rise among positivistic men who thought truth was relative, but among men who believed in self-evident and eternal verities." (note 21)

Laird next contrasts these philosophical assumptions with those of communism. Communism is not only relativistic and positivistic, it is a peculiar mixture of realistic calculation that will back off when confronted with a superior force and irrational dogma that commits it to inevitable, if postponed, conflict. It is this insidious force that we must confront, and says Laird, quoting Charles Malik favorably, "what is at stake in this . . . is the traditional view of man, society, history, truth and God which the Mediterranean-European-Western world has painstakingly developed over four thousand years of history." (note 22) Time is not on our side. "Time, to the extent that we do not use it in furthering our own cause and perfecting our own strengths, buys for the enemy the needed days, months, and years in which to catch up and eventually, if unimpeded, surpass us. . . . In the next few years, conceivably, we could move into the perilous phase of nuclear parity." (note 23) To prevent this we must educate the people as to the true nature of the values we defend and the true character of the enemy, and we must as well mobilize the economic, military, managerial, and technological resources required to maintain the initiative. Indeed we must serve credible notice "that we reserve to ourselves the initiative to strike first when the Soviet peril point rises beyond its tolerable limit." (note 24) Nor can the technological superiority that we now possess give us much comfort. In the name of all that is holy, we must continue to move ahead ceaselessly: our margin *"cannot protect us from technological breakthroughs!* [Laird's italics] . . . We must understand the Soviet strategy for what it is, and realize that the technological battleground is the decisive arena of the Cold War." (note 25) To support this national purpose, a strong domestic economy, a strong standing military force, and advances in weapons systems are required. Civilization and the urban ethos, indeed, God's will, demand them.

The "moderate" perspective of McNamara is much less explicitly ideological and quasi-theological. But there are similar strains running through his book, even if they resound in a new key. He too is calling the public to a thoughtful debate; (note 26) he too sees that "principles and philosophy" by which the defense establishment is governed are crucial; (note 27) and he too sees that the actions which are taken "affect not only the security, but the very survival of our twentieth century society. Fundamentally, what is at issue today, as it was a decade ago and as it will be a decade from now, is the kind of world in which we and others wish to live." (note 28) But, in contrast to Laird, that world is not defined by appeal to eternal principles, but by appeal to other more universal constructs than national ego-centrism. The basis of defense is the hope "of helping to create, in keeping with the principles of the United Nations Charter, a world in which even the smallest state could look forward to an independent existence, free to develop in its own way, unmolested by its neighbors, and free of fear of armed attack or political domination by the more powerful nations." (note 29) One finds order, thus, not in the nature of things; but in a pluralistic, international commonality that is based on the voluntary participation in collective defense. "Right order" is less the point of reference than "viable order" by developing interlocking alliances and mutual interdependencies that sustain and extend the boundaries of freedom. "This does not mean that we must assume the role of world policeman," he writes, "but it does mean that we must be willing to continue to support those international arrangements which help to preserve world peace, alleviate conflicts among nations, and create conditions for economic and social progress in the less developed areas of the world." (note 30)

Nor does McNamara understand communism as a monolithic enemy. There are fissures in the communist camp between Russia and China especially that as yet show no sign of healing. Indeed, our interests have not fared badly as a result. Still, realism "bids us both to seek understanding with them and to recognize that, in some areas at least, they remain fundamentally hostile to us despite their own differences." (note 31) They continue to refuse to let their ideology compete freely in the political marketplace and insist on trying to extend its influence by subversion and military pressure. Hence, it must be restrained by maintaining a full range of flexible responses in the context of multilateral agreements in the "free world."

Most notably, the defense establishment must face the necessity of planning and preparation "against the possibility of thermonuclear war." (note 32) The cornerstone of our policy is deterrence by "assured destruction capability." That is, of having the capability, even after a surprise nuclear attack on our cities, our industries, on our population, and on our retaliatory forces and command apparatus, of "damaging the aggressor to the point that his society would be simply no longer viable in twentieth century terms. . . . It means the certainty of suicide to the aggressor, not merely to his military forces, but to his society as a whole." (note 33) McNamara goes on to show that although the United States has a margin of superiority in nuclear weaponry, at present neither the Soviet Union nor the United States possesses the capacity to destroy the other's "assured destruction capability," so that the world is at a state of mutual deterrence. And it is this that "provides us both with the strongest possible motive to avoid a nuclear war." (note 34)

In contrast to Melvin Laird, who felt that superiority of nuclear weaponry should render the United States a kind of initiative which we would have to maintain, Robert McNamara argues for the sustaining of a kind of parity and points out that "superiority of weapons today does not effectively translate into political control or diplomatic leverage." (note 35) We are not freed by military superiority to "roll back" any political, economic, or ideological force we oppose, for we cannot use the military trump card without risking what we stand for as well as destroying what we oppose. Nor need we fret unduly about some dramatic technological breakthrough that would put us behind. "We do not want a nuclear arms race with the Soviet Union, primarily because the action-reaction phenomenon makes it foolish and futile. But if the only way to prevent the Soviet Union from obtaining first strike capability over us is to engage in such a race, the United States possesses in ample abundance the resources, the technology, and the will to run faster in that race for whatever distance is required." (note 36) Nevertheless, our preference would be for negotiated agreements to limit or reduce military preparation.

Whether we have to engage in continual preparation or are able to come to reasonable agreement, our responsibility under God is to exercise our human capacities by organized planning, by management. It is that which can preserve us from chaos; it is that through which social, political, and economic change is rationally extended in society.

"Some critics today worry that our democratic free societies are becoming overmanaged. . . . As paradoxical as it may sound, the real threat to democracy comes not from overmanagement, but from undermanagement. To undermanage reality is not to keep it free. It is simply to let some force other than reason shape reality. That force may be unbridled emotion; it may be greed; it may be aggressiveness; it may be hatred; it may be ignorance; it may be inertia; it may be anything other than reason. But whatever it is, if it is not reason that rules man, then man falls short of his potential." (note 37)

Finally, McNamara places the whole discussion in the context of new awareness that must be taken into account. The current protest against rationality and bureaucratized institutions is appreciated as a possible symbolization of the renaissance of metaphysics and a heralding of new concerns for democratic participation. But he resists the tendencies to characterize complex organizations as depersonalized, Orwellian nightmares, since ". . . it is possible that exactly the reverse is the case . . . , that democracy can become non-participating precisely to the degree that organic and hierarchical management breaks down." (note 38) Simplicity of organization is not by definition superior to complexity, as we can see in the chaos of cities without good management, in the brontosaurus with his tiny inadequate brain, and in the Adam and Eve story where a simple arrangement led to "an extraordinary amount of difficulty." If we are going to deal with those problems that engender hostility, poverty, poor education, lack of skills, underdevelopment—we must develop adequate tools to deal with them. In modern society, security means development and development requires bureaucratized coordination for planning and mobilization of resources. (note 39) Civilization, humanity, and the urban ethos require it.

These two official spokesmen for and managers of the Military-Industrial Complex diverge on many points, as we have seen. And these differences are of tremendous practical political importance. But there are some notable points of coincidence. They both presuppose conflict and disorder as the state of human affairs. One attempts to overcome this by return to ontologically given "right order," the other by pragmatic working out of agreements by rational management. Both see modern, urban, technological society as the highest achievement of man, and both call for mobilization of the skills of that society to preserve it. Both find it necessary to contemplate total destruction of society if a counter-society with comparable capacities, but with different interests and ideologies, challenges it. Laird hints at a preemptive strike to accomplish this and even toys with the political slogan "Better dead than red." McNamara is clearly concerned only with counterstrike capabilities, but presupposes a judgment that any society that strikes at ours must suffer the consequences of being reduced to a pre-modern society. Both appeal to the ultimate rational capacities of man and see them as given in divine responsibility, to be exercised in a hardheaded, disciplined calculus of risk and possibility. And both agree that we are dealing with fundamentally normative questions of what man ought to be and become.

In short, despite the divergences at every level, the Military-Industrial Complex is not only a social matrix, and not only a social phenomenon rooted in an historical process of a century's duration; it is also a value system of goals, purposes,

and assumptions about man, society, and history which is articulated and defined by its leadership. It is a subculture that is as
distinctive as the other subcultures of American life. It is, to be
sure, not only a social-historical matrix of institutions as we saw
at the conclusion of the previous chapter; but it also involves a
value-laden interpretation of reality. The Military-Industrial
Complex is also a mind-set built on unprovable assumptions.
It is a faith, a quasi-theology. It contains a social-psychological
set of common goals, purposes, and assumptions that approach
a world-view. At each level, it is inextricably tied to groups,
subcultures and ideologies that are marginal to it, but upon
which it relies and depends for political support. It is, nevertheless, within itself the para-society of modern life. Like the
church in medieval society, it provides a more cosmopolitan
definition of the human situation than do other institutions,
more opportunity for upward mobility, training, education, and
responsibility than other, wholly civilian, structures, a more
universal outlook of service to man and God than is available
in the ordinary "job," and a sense of working with life and death
issues. At the same time, no other institution or set of institutions in the society has the skills, communication networks,
know-how, and resources to deal with social stresses and international conflict so fully. And as the medieval church came into
influence through the chaos of Roman political ineptitude and
exterior pressure, the Military-Industrial Complex came to frui-
tion in response to a need for social coordination and planning
at a time when other vehicles for these purposes were politically impossible because of anti-communist and antisocialist
sentiment. The Military-Industrial Complex began to assume
many responsibilities for economic and social betterment (including regional economy, racial integration, new forms of public education, government supported medical and natural-
science research, and so on) that could not be dealt with in the
open political forum.

But there are decisive differences between the role of
the church in the Middle Ages and the structure of medieval
society that make the analogy only partially pertinent. Both the

social structure and its value structures have changed. Instead of a feudal society based on land and agriculture, we are, as has been repeatedly suggested, dealing with an urban, technological, corporative society that is on the one hand oligarchical and on the other ruled by consent of the governed. And instead of a cosmological, speculative, and traditional catholic frame of reference, we are living in a value setting primarily influenced by semi-secularized forms of the Magisterial Reformation, particularly by its Calvinistic forms.* Contrary to much current superficial criticism of Max Weber's *The Protestant Ethic and the Spirit of Capitalism* there is a well-documented relation of Protestantism to modern technological, commercial, and industrial life, and to a secularization process that organizes, bureaucratizes, rationalizes, quantifies, and calculates relative risks. This realistic-visionary mix *has* resulted in, and has, I believe, actually reached its zenith in, the para-society of the Military-Industrial Complex. It is now the shadow side of the Protestant world-view which in its semi-secularized form has become the operating assumptions of Jew, Catholic, humanist—and communist, too.

This para-society, with its distinctive spectacles for perceiving the world, is both creative and destructive. There is no doubt that (like the efforts to build the pyramids or ziggurats in the ancient Near East, or to build the cathedrals in Medieval Europe) the Military-Industrial Complex is a technological and organizational feat that cannot be matched in contemporary life. It is also true, however, that the essential purpose of this complex remains to prepare for destruction, and that its perception of reality has shown evidence of distortion in Viet Nam. Every civilization uses its technology in three ways: to build new forms of civilization, to construct artifacts for eternity, or to build arms to attack or defend against counter-civilizations or counter-symbols of eternity. Functionally, if not always inten-

* The term *Magisterial Reformation* refers to that of Luther, Calvin, and their adherents; and is usually contrasted with the Radical Reformation of both the sectarians on the continent and the Cromwellian Revolution in England.

tionally, the Complex is caught in the irony of its own situation. It uses the highest civilizational forms and the highest symbols of eternality for attack and defense alone. To defend democracy, it finds, internally, the suspension of the democratic system necessary; to defend technological superiority, it mobilizes technology to destroy counter-technologies; to protect the urban ethos, it targets cities; to garner the funds to extend "urbane" styles of life, it devours funds for the cities. It has provided much stimulus to new forms of human imagination, to cosmopolitan outlooks, and to new forms of social cooperation. But the imagination is focused on weapons systems, the cosmopolitan world becomes divided into friends and enemies, and the social cooperation becomes a relatively closed subculture which the host culture cannot fully understand.

Finally, this complex, the new secular papacy, has the ear of the court. It identifies the situation, defines its perimeters, invokes values, suggests solutions, combines and interprets information, and generates means in a highly effective way. For all its bumbling and red tape, no other institution in society has the capacity to do what it does in so effective a way. And these functions must be performed. The political decision-makers require it and depend on it. The population at large allows it to continue because matters are so complicated for the layman and the Military-Industrial Complex continually supplies the public, through a multiplicity of channels, with categories and facts, perspectives and particulars, that are otherwise unavailable. Strong residues of anti-socialism legitimate the assumptions of the Military-Industrial Complex and prevent the building of other complexes for constructive ends. Both political leadership and the people at large leave it to the experts. Only when the experts become divided, as in the ABM dispute, is some serious debate possible in limited spheres.

The result is an ethic of necropolis—an urbanized ethos at the center of technological civilization that appears both to be necessary for its preservation and to be the bearer of its death and destruction, the netherworld of Protestantized modern society. The most influential interpretation of the overarching values of Western society and the specific inner logic of the

Complex are linked in a quasi-theology that unintentionally portends the death of the urban ethos, the destruction of the city, and irrational sacrifice to a rationalized, cosmopolitan Deity upon which it was based.

CHAPTER FIVE

The foundations of transformation

The critique of any large social system that claims quasi-theological legitimacy must begin in the critique of its religion. On this point, theologians, philosophers, and social theorists in the traditions of Weber or Marx can agree. The Military-Industrial Complex is, at its core, guided by a set of presuppositions of a metaphysical nature that shape its philosophy of history, its definitions of good and evil, and its specific interpretations of cultural values. If the core problem of the Military-Industrial Complex is valuational and quasi-theological, the several levels of the moral and theological issues must be sorted and brought under scrutiny in order to see what can and what should be transformed.

In the first place, the Complex invokes theological symbols in its final appeal for legitimacy. Supporters and critics of the Complex frequently rest their cases on questions of ultimate loyalty and on assessments of what is worthy of that loyalty. And whether their perspectives are consciously informed by concepts of God, as are Melvin Laird's and those of many Pacifists, or whether there are substitute terms for that which is conceived as ultimately powerful and worthy of loyalty (which the tradition has called God), is basically irrelevant. Points of appeal to the ultimate condition of mankind are made in all the major perspectives, employing a world view that is theological even when not theistic. To be theological, in this broad sense, is part and parcel of human reflection on ultimate matters. It is, I believe, part of the arrogance of theologians that they presume no one else is asking or answering such questions, just as it is the arrogance of military personnel to assume that no one else is interested in security or defense because the language, the level of abstraction, the kinds of precedents appear to differ. Insofar as the Military-Industrial Complex is asking such questions in its mode of operations and value assumptions, we are dealing with a theological matter of some substance and it is the responsibility of theologically concerned ethicists to inquire into the adequacy of such interpretations.

The Military-Industrial Complex presents an additional theological problem in the sense that life and death, good and evil, salvation or destruction contend vigorously throughout its workings. These matters have always been among the chief concerns of theology, and depend finally on theological-like judgments even if posed in quite different terms. They now are thrust upon the synagogues and churches with a new urgency, not from the intrinsic development of their "messages," but from the world that has at least partly burst out of their bounds of influence.

Closely related is the fact that the modern urban, technological society that produced the Military-Industrial Complex and its parallels in Germany, South Africa, and Russia is deeply imbued with underlying values developing out of the Protestant ethic. Without the work ethic and its rationalizing-bureaucratizing processes of management and production, its willingness to transform nature for the sake of "higher" loyalties, and its correlative citing of empirical success as evidence of a providentially initiated, higher calling, the society which has hatched these institutions would be inconceivable. These values derive from Calvinist sources historically and were developed in multiple religious and secular settings as a quite serious this-worldly-asceticism. Such motifs are now built into both the host society and its militant child.

Thus, in at least three senses, the core of the Military-Industrial Complex bears theological import; and these meanings suggest that man needs some ultimate justifying frame of reference in order to develop or modify life-styles and institutions. Hence, if man is to modify, control, or compromise the Military-Industrial Complex, he must develop an alternative justifying frame of reference. He must theologically reconceptualize the Complex.

Finally, the Military-Industrial Complex is a theological

problem in that it attempts to find an ultimate security through totalization of human power to defend the present and assure the future. But from a theological perspective, a perspective supported by considerable empirical evidence, final security is never a human possibility. The attempt absolutely to secure the future leads to a ritualized compulsiveness that becomes instead a tyranny over the future—as can be seen in psychiatry, sociology, and politics as well as in religion. Security, instead, must be seen in terms of commitment to human development, as McNamara suggests. But such a commitment requires a theological dimension that he does not articulate. We must develop a vision of future possibility which liberates us from our frantic attempts to assure security in the present by the compulsive defensiveness that seems to be a part of our religio-cultural heritage. A broader vision of a new cosmopolis must be invoked. In that vision, the possibility of fulfilling and transforming human existence becomes a source of security that transcends compulsive defensiveness and engenders a capacity to risk and trust.

One must not, however, be naïve about the possibility. Premature plunges into the future entail their own pathologies, as we have previously suggested in regard to Pacifism and Holy War. The realities of the human situation demand a routine security that establishes the accomplishments of the past and defends them from challenge so that man's life is not preoccupied with survival and so that he can seek an existence of quality and meaning. The problems occur when the realistic need for routine security becomes a ritualized, compulsive quest for guarantees, and when defense becomes polarized against a vision of improbable danger. Apocalyptic policy is then a serious temptation. That is a theological motif of fundamental significance.

In spite of frequent distortions and parochialisms in interpretation, the God of the Judeo-Christian tradition stands in contrast to the presumed God of the Military-Industrial Complex. The power worshiped by the Complex does not have the power of salvation for man; and the worth valued by the Complex is only partially worthy of human loyalty. For the God of the tradition is focused upon a just peace, which cannot finally depend upon, although it sometimes must rely temporarily upon, even the just employment of war to guide the common life.

The God of Abraham, Isaac, and Jacob is a covenant-forming God. He continually enters into the stuff of history to bring about new combinations and senses of peoplehood with a sense of obligation to the whole of humanity. And he draws his people not from the powerful, but from the oppressed. He calls them out of oppression and provides them with a promise of the means of sustenance. And those who oppose them by an increasing mobilization of instruments for war become mired in the mud. The exodus of peoples from economic and political servitude and the formation of covenants of justice and equity are only conceived as acts of impiety by those who worship dead gods.

That God, who is also the God of Jesus, calls man no longer to suffer under the tyranny of the fear of death, nor to worship legalistic, financial, or political realities as finally authoritative. Through man's willingness to take upon himself the suffering of others, God promises a quality and shape of life beyond immediate structures that pragmatic calculation cannot articulate or anticipate.

And when the believers in that same God confronted imperial power (at least when they first had occasion to affect it in any fashion, during the days of Constantine), they not only rearticulated the responsibility of believers for political righteousness, they properly stated that God was not to be found in monolithic structures or single-centered complexes, nor in a multiplicity of independent centers of loyalty. Instead, God becomes concrete to man in pluralistic structures. They developed, therefore, the often confusing doctrine of the trinity.

During the Middle Ages, in the perennial conflicts of church and state, Catholic believers in this same pluralistically experienced God struggled vigorously to maintain a fundamental principle that the divine is never fully resident in temporal power. Social-political systems are, they claimed, of fundamental concern; but the structures which hold the sword are, in the final analysis, temporary and not eternal. They can be changed, and they must appeal to principles extrinsic and not intrinsic to themselves to claim legitimacy.

The Protestants of the Reformation understood that this same God required continual protest against institutions that pretended to have exclusive rights to mediate the power of salvation to man. No single institution can be trusted with such power, and hence man must construct counter-institutions to perform similar tasks in new situations and to compromise the claims of self-perpetuating outmoded ideologies.

More recently, the Abolition, "Social Gospel," "Realist," "Post-Hitler Jewish," "Vatican II Catholic," and "Black power" theologians have understood that same God as demanding the extension of cosmopolitan patterns of life to all peoples through the implementation of both political and economic democracy. They face the frustration of a world in which relative political democracy is confronting relative economic democracy in an apparently intensifying, apocalyptic struggle.

Each of these ingredients in the historic interpretation of the God of the Judeo-Christian tradition was accompanied by secondary and tertiary themes which, when made dominant, led to pathological religious and social movements. Hence the bearers of the theological vision come continually under theological critique themselves. But in our situation, when the chief bearer of a distorted quasi-theology in the West is the Military-Industrial Complex, it becomes necessary to bring the resources of the tradition to bear against the worship of gods who are no gods as they are evident in contemporary policy.

For the sake of clarity, it must be stated that this book makes no claims at this point about the metaphysical status of any divine beings, although a full systematic treatment might require such articulation. The claim it makes here is much more limited: that in several crucial moments of the Judeo-Christian tradition, described above, man has made theological-ethical decisions which, whether one can accept or even tolerate the specific metaphysical language or ontological assumptions attending them or not, are nonetheless proper decisions. Specifically, it claims that no conception of ultimate worth and no interpretation of ultimate power is legitimate that does not focus upon these dimensions and possibilities of life; and that contrasting presumptions about the state of man, the world, and political life are not worthy of human loyalty. And finally, since God-talk claims that something universal is at stake, this book claims that the non-theistic humanist would, upon reflection, have to come to conceptions of power and worth that are functionally similar to the specific symbol-clad claims of the tradition.

Now, if an adequate theological conception is to be found in such claims, how adequate is the quasi-theological position of the Military-Industrial Complex and its commitment to the contemporary distortion of the urban ethos into necropolis?

The primary values of the urban ethos are specific versions of the theological-ethical norms derived from this heritage, norms perhaps best articulated through concepts of freedom and order: freedom from the bondages of past tyranny and natural necessity, and freedom for technological and planned transformation of the future toward a new commonwealth by responsible utilization of the gifts of nature and the geopolitics of present patterns; order that is pluralistic and open, yet order disciplined and integrated by voluntary agreement, duty, and tolerance in a covenant of mutual obligation whose source and destiny escape empirical detection. The Military-Industrial Complex has appropriated these goals, as well as the technological-managerial skills to manipulate people and material to these ends, from the urban ethos—but its efforts have produced three ironies of major significance.

First, as already stated, a complex designed to secure modified, urban capitalism has passed beyond the structure of that capitalism into a corporative communitarianism for those within the fold of the Military-Industrial Complex, with birth-to-death governmental support, governmental services at every hand, government-managed employment and education possibilities, and at least implicit loyalty to governmental objectives as a prerequisite to promotion. Thus, a form of modified socialism, populated by the rich whose loyalties are to uncommon wealth and noncommonwealth, is called upon to protect an outmoded form of individual entrepreneurship among all, including the poor, at home and abroad. In fact, individual entrepreneurship functions only among the poor and the marginal; for the great corporations, the unions, the universities, and the Military-Industrial Complex itself are in large measure communitarian and socialistic in structure and function. Thus a concentration of economic life is defended by an instrument contrary to its ideology. But that conception does not itself operate in the decisive centers of power. Independent, individualistically based institutions, even if they made up 90 percent of the society, could not compete, in defining problems, mobilizing resources, and solving problems, with a coordinated, technologically competent, marginal 10 percent.

Second, the military arrangements made to defend and secure the urban centers as essential for the preservation of modern society are related to the methods used to threaten the enemies' urban centers. And other countries have taken the same steps. Now a situation exists in which, on the basis of the values of urban-technological society, no urban-technological center can be secured. No military power on the face of the earth can now do what it is called to do: guarantee defense and security for the decisive population and institutional centers. Now only by threat of retaliatory action, namely, by targeting second-strike forces against presumed enemies' cities can the partial, tenuous security of threat and intimidation delay attack against the cities. But no one can today defend or secure the city; he can only destroy two for one.

And finally, reliance on security and defense has brought insecurity and indefensibility by failing to apply to the values themselves the hard-headed calculus of risk proper to the military establishment. How much security and how much defense ought society to have? Recent administrations have answered that question by the doctrine of "sufficiency," and by reduction of military visibility. Yet it appears that security, whether by its own name or by the name of sufficiency, still means dominance—a false meaning of the term theologically or politically. The specification of the extent of "sufficiency" cannot be left to the Complex itself and to its allies. There it is only interpreted in terms of the quasi-theology and the given value system. Such a decision cannot be left to those whose overriding professional responsibility is security against every and all real, imagined, or potential threats. Their answer is necessarily "complete" security or "assured" defense. Ordinary political observation indicates that trying to develop a riskless political-military power capability carries pathological risks, both because the attempt serves as an invitation to tyranny and because it constricts the vision of human need to one area so that the plurality of needs tends to be ignored. And the Judeo-Christian tradition has, with few exceptions, warned against the theological and moral dangers of seeking complete assurance of eternally guaranteed existence. Life is to be lived toward a future transformation involving both fulfillment and judgment of present life and not merely in terms of defense of the present. And the attempt is contrary to belief in a transcendent center of power and worth that can never be fully appropriated in this life. The most striking portraits of hell are reserved in the literature of the tradition for those who attempted to secure absolute power in the present under the pretense of valid goals. The awareness of such temptations has deeply influenced much religious and ethical pacifism and anti-militarism to ignore the realistic need for relative security and defense.

How much security and defense is needed can only be arrived at by a calculation of the multiplicity of needs and threats in proportion to the available resources and in relation to the relative worth of what is being made secure and defended. The implications of this assumption are twofold. On the one hand, the definition of overall needs and threats cannot remain in the hands of one group professionally structured to define only one set of needs and certain kinds of threats. It must be a political-moral, a statesmanlike, definition that effectively represents the whole range of human needs. On the other, a moral assessment of the moral worth of that which is being made secure and defended is required. The Military-Industrial

Complex, especially as its value assumptions are exemplified in the statements of Melvin Laird, is incapable of making that assessment. Appeals to eternal truths, God, self-evident realities that are treated as transcending the human situation are also treated as totally manifest in the present social system. This view is incapable of value-oriented self-criticism. The ultimate loyalties of the militant "denomination" of the Military-Industrial Complex are based on too-unambiguous a division of good and evil, and are identified with "we" and "they." Such cosmic dualism tends also to obscure other kinds of human and social needs and to make other needs subservient to the battle of the titans that will surely come. Theologically and ethically, no nation can legitimately lay claim to such purity nor attribute such totally demonic power to other centers of human loyalty.

The more pragmatic "denominationalism" inside the Military-Industrial Complex, exemplified by Robert McNamara, has a higher degree of theological and moral validity precisely in its recognition that *mutual* restraint among nations is valid and that extension of areas of *mutual* agreement and *mutual* interest is morally and politically required. After all, we have lived in the world with communism for quite some time and we can probably live with it longer. It really is not so strikingly different from other ideologically based nationalisms. And it has much more in common with the Judeo-Christian tradition—especially in its demand for economic democracy—than many like to admit. Further, McNamara, like many moderates in the Complex, is deeply concerned about other kinds of human needs. Questions of urban reconstruction, reduction of racism, new directions in education, medical research, and poverty alleviation, were all part of the moderate military horizon. As mentioned earlier, these concerns were in part foisted upon the Military-Industrial Complex because the whole society has been, during much of the century of development of the Complex, so obsessed with anticommunism that it refused to appropriate sufficient funds to deal with common problems. Only by interpreting these problems as threats to the national capacity to resist communism and handling them under the auspices of the Department of Defense or the CIA could the United States legitimately address them. However, these were always left-handed functions of the Complex, and when it came to a show-down regarding conceptions of security and defense in the Viet Nam conflict, the Military-Industrial Complex honored its first obligations to other concerns and definitions of needs. The inner logic of the military establishment does not allow it to become primarily a social agency. Thus was evoked an enormous hostility toward the Military-Industrial Complex on the part of those within and without who had most intensively worked on problems of urban reconstruction, education, racism, disease, and poverty. The critics turned not only against the Complex, but against the managerial-technological approach to problems in an occasionally frenzied, paranoiac, often neo-Luddite, sys-tems-smashing mood that sometimes was imagined as growing out of an alliance with "the enemy," communism.

The political-ethical dilemmas that grew from the false theology of the Complex and the reinterpretation of urban-technological values in its terms and in terms of the particular values of the military (security and defense) are still with us and present at least four major problems in contemporary dis-cussion. Indeed, these are in modified and recast forms the same problems that are raised more crudely by the romantic, the localist, the universalist, and the reactionary interpretations of political ideology (see chapter 1). The first dilemma is that although society needs security and defense, acquiring the in-struments and social mechanisms necessary to them weakens its sensitivity to other needs. The possibilities for a just peace are not likely to be found in a commonwealth preoccupied by security and defense at the expense of concerns for urban re-construction and the human problems of ignorance, racism, disease, environmental pollution, and poverty. Indeed, security must be defined as including defenses against these enemies. But McNamara's suggestions notwithstanding, these cannot be dealt with by a military defense establishment or else, when the chips are down, concerns for a just peace will perennially be subordinated to concerns for war. Security and defense, then, must not be abandoned; but they must not be allowed to singularly or even largely govern the urban technological skills which could be applied to other areas. Indeed, if viable at all in the long run, they must become subordinate to the total definition of needs and threats in the society and abroad.

At this point, however, we are confronted by an apparent conflict between obligations to provide for survival and the obligations to provide for the quality of life. Does not the very fact of life take precedence over its quality? Does not the *esse* precede the *bene esse?* And does not, therefore, provision for the defense of the society take priority over provision for the niceties of liberty and equity, culture and affluence? Are not the latter possible only if the former is secured? In one sense, the answer is an obvious yes. Life itself must go on if it is to be significant. But from other perspectives, the answer must be no. That is not our situation, and to say that it is distorts perception of the alternatives before us. Is it not likely that the promotion of liberty and equity, culture and affluence at home and abroad would reduce the threats to domestic and foreign attacks on the society? Even if we had to choose between survival and a life of quality, it is not at all clear that the present definitions of security could really secure, and the present definitions of defense really defend. And, from explicitly moral perspectives, we must ask whether a society that does not provide for liberty and equity, culture and distribution of affluence for the public need is worthy of defense and security. In short, then, there may be no hierarchy of values implemented in the policies of a society which subordinates the questions of the quality of life to flat definitions of survival and defense. The society that is not dedicated to the quality of life may not govern life itself. On this point the romantics have a legitimate criticism of society.

Second, despite the tendency of the Complex to distort humanistic and democratic values, we must resist our own tendency to oppose the technological-managerial approach to problems just because this is the way the Military-Industrial Complex approaches them. Dispersed structures of authority and decision-making are, in one sense, a necessary correlate of the bigness of urban-technological society, and necessary to diversity. Multitudinous decisions cannot be made efficiently by the few at the top, although the few may try to preserve their prerogatives. But a case can be made that good technological-managerial approaches to problems require, in today's context, increased lower-level independence. The higher-level organizational functions must become more and more limited to funding, quality control, and coordination rather than direction. Wider ranges of local organization, authority, and experimentation can be exercised within a nondirective, supportive, and regulative context. This seems to be true in public education, public transportation, urban renewal, ecclesiastical organization, and corporation management. Where it is not, immense hostilities are generated. Hence, modern technological-managerial capabilities allow regular appeals to lower levels of decision-making that can partially replace the more common practice of appealing up the ladder of organization. But the necessity for addressing large-scale social problems by efficient large-scale social complexes cannot be denied. The problem is that only the Military-Industrial Complex is operating effectively at the present time. That is, only that set of institutions is maintaining coordinated control of budgetary resources, defining the alternatives for national policy, and, even though it has promoted inefficient military and social behavior, is holding divergent groups in an integrated structure of social solidarity. The tendency of radicals and, often, of liberals to flee, resist, or intentionally attempt to destroy technological-managerial organization *in principle,* just because particular forms of it have to be opposed in practice, is evidence of a kind of corrupt romanticism that bears the seeds of destruction for man and society. Directly, it undercuts the human capacity to solve large-scale human problems that are malleable only to large-scale mobilization of resources. Indirectly, it leaves the field open to the manipulations of those who have fewer humanitarian and social concerns but extensive technical, managerial, and organizational skills. And throughout, it prevents the routinizing of lower-level tasks so that enough people are freed from drudgery to ask questions of meaning, policy, and orientation which could improve the quality of life. The urban-technological values of freedom from the past and freedom from the necessities of nature, of freedom for a new commonwealth, are the only path toward a just peace. Only by voluntarily joining in the duties and tolerances of the urban-technological life can the liberal and even radical concerns become actual possibilities. The problem is that the romantics have left that path to others because it seemed too rationalistic for them, and others have trod it because it seemed the only road to avoid or defeat communism. It has been thus preempted in the name of war, even of Just War, instead of Just Peace. But a reinterpretation of localism in terms of diffused, pluralistic authority can become a counterweight to such temptation.

Third, and closely related to the above, is the nature of the world situation we are in. There is no doubt that exterior threats to our existence from the communist world could develop. It is altogether likely that Russia and possibly China have Military-Industrial Complexes with goals, purposes, and assumptions toward the United States similar to those the United States has about them. And there is surely a denominational split between the militants and moderates in those countries that is comparable to the situation here, with both living in a common subculture which is committed to its own perpetuation, both working on the forefront of technological and managerial skills, and both having more than ordinary access to the ears of decision-makers. So long as such complexes exist elsewhere, and are not subject to international regulation, some sort of limited complex will be required here to keep the patterns of international mutual restraint alive. And that complex must be prepared to counter challenges to security, even though present over-preparedness makes this argument almost unnecessary. But by extending the range of responsibility of the Military-Industrial Complex to include such concerns as urban reconstruction, education, racism, health, and poverty in the name of defense, we not only obscure its proper ends of military security and defense, but we reduce the possibility of development in all the other spheres. The taking of risks in aid to the third world, the exploration of technological-managerial possibilities in civilian arenas where it could become tied to new forms of democratic participation in decision-making; the building of coordinated links for contracting, research, and development—these are all interpreted in the confining perspective of a possible East-West conflict. The Military-Industrial Complex, thus, must be constrained to perform its proper ends, and to free the resources to develop other viable ends in other ways.

The institutions, skills, and linkages of the Military-Industrial establishment, domestic and foreign, have actually contributed to the development of structures of modern society that make the communist-capitalist debates irrelevant. They are vestiges of the past with, to be sure, enormous emotional investments and considerable political mileage, but they are pre-urban, pre-technological socio-fictions that have no more pertinence than nineteenth century novels about moon-men in a day of walking on the moon. Ethically, it is necessary to de-mythologize and de-ideologize the confrontation of complexes. It is equally necessary to recognize the relative superiority of the crucial dimensions of the West's political democracy and the relative superiority of selected ingredients of the East's economic democracy that promote justice and equity as a precondition of peace. The West cannot, in de-mythologizing, however, compromise on its understanding of the necessity for some recognizable form of political democracy, although it need not be in the mold of John Locke. It is still unprovable but also still not refutable to argue that in the long run it is more likely that economic democracy appropriate to an urban-technological society that sustains a higher quality of life can be promoted from a political democratic base than that political democracy in any genuine sense can be promoted from an economic democratic base. The preservation of political democracy and the striving for economic democracy can, nevertheless, only be accomplished by subordinating security and defense to the larger goals and possibilities of modern society. Security and defense must become subservient to a more universal vision of just peace instead of the other way around.

The fourth dilemma is centered in the extensive and complicated purposes which bind men's lives into the life of the Complex. As previously suggested, there are many ways in which military, research, development, labor, and business personnel find meaning, as well as occupations and financial support, for their lives in working on the forefront of technical, managerial, and production projects for the sake of the national welfare. At the same time their horizons do not always include an understanding of the consequences of their actions nor a sense of responsibility for the whole shape of things. Quite understandably, people tend to focus only on immediate reality. There is some evidence that this is changing. Scientists who helped develop the atomic bomb became deeply concerned about the consequences and founded the *Bulletin of Atomic Scientists* some time ago. The appearance on several Army bases of "underground newspapers" raising questions about military structure and policy is a modest, but significant fact. Recent student and faculty "teach-ins" and demonstrations at the M.I.T., Johns Hopkins, and Southern California research centers indicate growing awareness and broadening of horizons in several key locations. The politicization of technologists during the ABM debate already suggests a trend that is likely to continue. And the reported purchase by the Pentagon of California grapes picked by strikebreakers precisely at the time when several of the major unions are becoming concerned about organizing migrant workers has begun to force organized labor to raise their eyebrows. But overall, the vast majority of military-industrial personnel either justify their actions by appeal to national service or do not examine their lives at all, living them in the narrow confines of job and family.

The consequences of this vocational parochialism which lends itself to valuational conservatism or even reaction are not unambiguous. In many respects, the Military-Industrial Complex has provided wider ranges of opportunity, loyalty, and meaning than would otherwise have been available. Sound values from our past *have* become part of people's lives through the presumedly "neutral" organizations of the Complex. And, it is also the case that in order to have a government that is at all responsive to the will of the people, a relatively neutral bureaucratic organization is a fundamental necessity. A governmentally controlled complex must not be so caught up in partisan positions that it cannot respond to policies that are contrary to its inclinations but are determined by democratic processes and issued by legitimate, superior authority. Thus, if it became the policy of the government, for example, to severely limit the defense budget, it would be necessary to have a sufficiently disengaged body of personnel who could interpret this policy in terms of the national welfare and who could, if necessary, find other, non-defense centers of employment and meaning without total disruption of their lives.

Thus, pragmatically, it is important to people and to democracy that institutions be arranged so that bureaucracies are obedient to the public will in a fashion that encourages the finding of meaning in public service as well as a pervasive sense of responsibility for the consequences of one's actions and the general shape of things. And, ethically, it becomes necessary to recover and re-accent a doctrine of vocations that makes each person conscious of professional service to a larger community in a way that does not destroy, but indeed, evokes a prophetic responsibility to discern the wider and deeper signs of the times and take responsibility for the overall structure and direction of society.

These four political-ethical dilemmas, then, all point toward a reordering of the values of the Military-Industrial Complex. Humanitarian concerns for a Just Peace must dominate a society willing to subordinate institutions of Just War; without ignoring genuine threats, the overarching values of defense and security must be defined by, and not remain the governing goals of, the urban-technological ethos; the assumed socio-fictions of communism versus capitalism locked in a cosmic struggle must be demythologized under a common quest for both economic and political democracy; the appropriateness of governmental guidance of pluralistically based authority must be recognized by modern urban society; and individual purposes must be expanded from purely personal meaning to include a wider sensitivity to the democratic responsibility for the social consequences of individual and corporate action.

These value transformations, however, cannot be accomplished by ethical reflection, preaching, or teaching alone. The present operating inner logic of the Military-Industrial value structure is related to a historical development that has, at least, century-long roots and to a matrix of social institutions that is highly developed. If we imagine the time, energy, money, and skills that have gone into the construction of the Military-Industrial Complex, we can get some idea of what is required to alter it. One cannot simply develop a self-conscious theological ethic for "secular preaching," continue to work with the same institutions, and then expect immediate widespread results any more than one can mount a soul-force attack against militarism, as is the wont of Pacifists, or call for a totally new set of revolutionized managers as demanded by contemporary radical crusaders.

Fortunately, the Judeo-Christian tradition, which in Protestant form deeply influenced modern, urban-technological society, and the two of them together, which allowed the distorted development of the partially necessary necropolis of the Military-Industrial Complex, have also produced other groups, institutions, skills, and linkages focused about other dominant goals utilized in the transvaluation of values. Indeed, the churches and synagogues, as divinely inspired and therefore self-appointed custodians of the values of mankind and traditionally concerned for their transformation, have, in spite of the reaction of many pious church people, and in the face of resistance from parishioners, entered into a series of alliances with various groups for precisely those purposes.

The Civil War, which demanded the immediate extension and full utilization of the Industrial Revolution and its managerial skills, also released a tenth of the population from slavery. That population, slowly and painfully, and with enormous societal and psychological hurdles, has begun to sensitize the nation to the needs of poverty groups throughout the country and to non-white people throughout the world, in alliance with the religious heirs of the abolition movement. The relatively untapped resources of this population with their passionate and even militant concerns for a just, equitable society and for the quality of life are now, in spite of some romantic temptations to withdraw into an isolated subculture, firmly in the forefront of efforts to question national priorities. Yet they are still systematically excluded from any large-scale participation in managerial-technological skills and institutions. Their inclusion in skill pools directed at upgrading the institutions of urban life, through federal funding and training comparable to that which for military purposes now accrues to other groups, would provide one basis for the national transvaluation of values.

The expanding economy after the Civil War which produced the giant corporations also produced a giant industrial labor force. The "Social Gospel" movement, which has parallels in Jewish, Catholic, and humanist movements of the late nineteenth and early twentieth centuries not only provided much of the ideology and leadership of the labor movement, but saw it as an attempt to redirect national policy toward concern for the quality of life not just for the few but for the many. The labor unions, even though they have now grown complacent on many issues and although they have sometimes become irrational bastions of racism and popular anti-communism, remain a major resource of skill, organization, and political power that is of fundamental importance. The dominant values of the movement remain brotherhood and justice and economic democracy through political democratic means; and the skills, though rusty, used to organize and mobilize large numbers of persons on the fringes of society so that they can move into the center of corporation policy-making through their representatives, are invaluable resources for the continued democratization of the economic system. No amount of contempt for them on the part of intellectual radicals, and no amount of exploitation of their sentiments by appeals to a "silent majority" to justify policies contrary to their interests and values will long succeed.

During the same period, the extension of public education, the passage of child-labor laws, and the urban, differentiated styles of family life allowed the development of an increasingly articulate youth culture. Given tremendous impetus after the World War II "baby boom," the youth themselves and the educational institutions that are stretched to capacity to care for them are providing another critical center of technical competence, organization, skill, and concern for the quality of urban-technological life in terms that refuse to subordinate these questions to defense and security. At the same time, they are sufficiently denied access to power that they can be critical of present institutions. Nothing is so dangerous as a disempowered intelligentsia.

The links between Black, poverty, labor, and youth groups, are still feeble and are threatened by divergent styles of life. But the population base, organizational skills, passions, and a growing political will are present for a coalition that could build an "Urban-Industrial Complex" to serve as a countervailing power to the Military-Industrial Complex; a passion for economic democracy to genuinely fulfill the promise of political democracy is a unifying theme. At present they lack coordination, funding, and linkages which, in all probability, will have to be built bit by bit from church, foundation, and private sources until they can gain the strength to claim governmental sources. The necessity of governmental involvement in these matters was established during the depression of the thirties and re-initiated in the now moribund "War on Poverty"; but it has never secured the sense of urgency that attends defense. Only the development of professional values and competence at leadership levels and massive efforts at local organization can lead to a viable set of institutions which could become linked and produce effective results.

The Spanish-American War initiated and World War I established, for the country, the necessity of becoming involved in entangling foreign alliances. World War II further accented that necessity and made it unavoidable for the United States to become a major figure on the world scene. The churches, at the same time, engaged in one of the largest missionary campaigns in the history of man, introducing modern forms of medicine, education, and faith, as well as strong vestiges of cultural imperialism, to underdeveloped countries. But the contemporary leaders, often the revolutionary ones, of the developing countries are products of the mission schools or recipients of church-sponsored scholarships to study in other countries. In secularized form, the creation of the United Nations acknowledged this new interdependence and the development of the Peace Corps was an extension of these universalizing drives. The corporations developed during this period also have extended their horizons internationally, sometimes bringing revolutionary changes by the introduction of western technology and values; sometimes bringing repression by supporting corrupt regimes economically or by neo-colonial tactics. Still, the indigenous technical and managerial personnel often received their training at the hands of the corporations. The result is a series of links to the developing countries that at present is officially presided over by the Department of State with close scrutiny from intelligence and military attachés. Yet the resources are present for new forms of a "Foreign-Industrial-Educational Complex" that, if carefully sensitized to indigenous values and if brought under alternative forms of cooperative supervision and control with the host peoples, could assist in the rapid development of these countries in a manner compatible with just peace. United Nations sponsorship, with United States funding (and perhaps that of other industrial nations), as well as indigenous control could provide a step to soften the imperialist and neo-colonial stances of present involvements and politicize, rather than militarize, the competition of the industrial nations vis-à-vis the third world.

The difficulty, of course, would be the building of a constituency to continually support such a program in domestic politics. But the involvement of 5 to 10 percent of the economy and labor force in such efforts could at least equal their present involvement in military projects. And, one would suspect, with far more likely results of a world-wide cosmopolis under a just peace.

Within the United States, a "Space-Industrial Complex" has grown up that is rooted in the same urban-industrial culture as the Military-Industrial Complex, but that has *partially* become independent of it. Initially engendered by fear of Russian space superiority, that complex has begun to take on its own distinctive stamp, develop its own links, traditions and values. Many concerned for urban problems or with international affairs find the expenditure on these projects adventurist and indicative of the failure of the nation to come to grips with human priorities. They have made their point so compellingly that a dull malaise pervades the space program at present. Should space exploration continue without fresh attempts at dealing with urban and foreign development, their suspicions may well be confirmed, and the spectacular achievements can be viewed only as the compulsive celebrations of the technological cult of a modern empire. But there are serious reasons why the space effort might well be continued.

In terms of domestic politics, it is necessary to have another matrix into which managerial-technical personnel can move. Their personal destinies should not be confined to the Military-Industrial Complex. Further, a large space team provides groups of governmental-industrial labor links outside the military, but with the necessary skills to evaluate the budgets and technical projects of the military. Indeed, they would, in many ways, compete with the Military-Industrial Complex for the same dollar and could provide critical, mutual evaluation of projects in terms other than those given by in-house proponents.

From the perspective of human values, the "Space-Industrial Complex" provides a vision of new horizons for man embracing the mystery of existence. Something in these efforts expands the soul. The statement by astronaut Armstrong as he began his walk on the moon, "That's one small step for a man, one giant leap for mankind," is a near-liturgical sentiment celebrating the humanization of the cosmos. In spite of the tendency of cynics to see the whole affair as a circus to divert national consciousness from its real problems, there is a kind of spiritual magnificence in the effort, the precise character and consequences of which are not yet clear. Should this complex be allowed to become the only alternative to the Military-Industrial

Complex, with one taking responsibility for the cosmos and the other for the world, the cynics will be proven correct. But that need not happen. International cooperation in space exploration could serve to mitigate earthly conflict. And if the "Space-Industrial Complex" becomes one in a whole repertoire of complexes to deal with the many dimensions of human needs and possibilities, it can play a highly significant role.

Finally, there has been a new surge of concern among the middle classes for ecology. Among contemporary causes, perhaps this is the most ambiguous. It contains motifs that echo pagan concerns for sacred groves and naturalistic deities. It might focus too much attention on saving fish and birds and not enough on people starving in poor communities. And there are neo-Luddite dimensions in some of these protests, too. But even this movement can become significant to the redefinition of human values if it focuses upon the democratic control of prime economic institutions in contrast to independent corporatism, if it defines the ecological systems in such a way that rats in the ghettoes are as much a concern as hummingbirds, if it promotes concern for the international eco-systems which involve the development of cross-cultural institutions and senses of common destiny, and if it develops new systems of non-polluting technological recycling.

In short, the transvaluation of values that have become inordinately dominated by the Military-Industrial Complex requires not only a shift in theological-ethical awareness. A substructure of social tissue is necessary to support value reconstruction. The construction of alternative complexes that are rooted in some of the same history and have a diversity of links and skills comparable to some aspects of the Military-Industrial Complex is necessary to weaken the destructive dimensions of the Complex. Merely clamping the lid on the military will, if previous history is our guide, only allow it to withdraw into itself, temporarily reduce its visibility, and harden its shell against the host culture without compromising its values, its structures, or its potential impact on national policy in times of crises. It may even resurrect militaristic outcries about a political "stab in the back." But the building of alternative complexes can provide an institutional base for alternative perspectives on the world and human responsibility in it. The first concern of those morally troubled by the power and policy of the Military-Industrial Complex might well be to begin the long, hard process of building counter-complexes that can restrain military power and reshape the polity of the nation.

CHAPTER SIX

Toward an ethic for a just peace

So far, it has been the contention of the foregoing chapters that the chief forms of moral discourse about public institutions of war are inadequate in the face of the Military-Industrial Complex. Usual forms of political ideology frequently fail to provide the mix of realistic and visionary dimensions of the human experience necessary for adequate moral guidance. They continually bog down in romanticism, localism, superficial internationalism, or reaction. In contrast, an effective mix of realism and vision is preserved in the historically evolving interpretations of God, which, together with the concept of a Just War, form the chief legacy of the Judeo-Christian tradition.

The Just War doctrine, which may run the gamut from righteous revolution to tactical or even nuclear pacifism, is a powerful and necessary moral tool in its own right. It deals almost entirely in matters of policy, however, and is rooted in an analogy between ethics and law. It therefore has little to say about matters of polity, in a day when international and domestic attentions are focused upon good order and the structure of power and authority. It also does not ask what categories are to be used to interpret the ethos. Indeed, as a set of universal principles, it transcends any situation and although it demands empirical analysis, it does not specify how that analysis shall take place.

Yet good order and a proper interpretation of the social-political situation affect how the principles of the Just War doctrine will be applied. A group of authors whom I called "secular preachers," men like Thomas Hayden, Gabriel Kolko, Richard Barnet, and John Kenneth Galbraith, *have* attempted to offer interpretations and provide visions of the possibilities.

And their efforts are among the more compelling available. However, they are all trying to deal with the idolatries of the "bureaucratic truths," with the condition of the soul of the nation, with the immoral structures of power that result, and with the need for conversion, without using theological or moral language. Perhaps these men have depended upon the social sciences for so long that to prove themselves "scientific" they have ruled out *a priori* dealing explicitly with values. But questions of ultimate power and worth have to be dealt with. Further, without a sense of the rootedness and continuities of social sin or grace, even in the face of massive social change, they confine their analyses for the most part to the immediate situation. They therefore bury some of the roots of the problem that extend back at least to the American Civil War and the Industrial Revolution. And finally, they see only indistinctly the intimate connections between the fundamental value structures of society, the Complex, and the loyalties of men. Hence their prescriptions for change do not provide a program that is both realistic and visionary, but instead appear rhetorical and propagandistic.

Therefore, an alternative interpretation of the Military-Industrial Complex has been developed, one which attempts to show that the social-historical roots of the Complex are deeper and more tangled than previously acknowledged; that in actual dimensions the Complex is not as extensive as frequently assumed; that resources are therefore available within the overall social system to confront it; and that forming its integrated core are certain confessional, quasi-theological elements. This interpretation calls upon man to assert fundamental theological and valuational norms to straighten out the Complex's perversion of valid urban-technological norms. Since values do not sustain themselves, it also calls for the development of counter-complexes that could provide alternatives to the Complex's definitions of human needs and threats and its prescriptions of the means and strategies for meeting them.

This analysis has been governed throughout by a concern for the development of an ethic of a Just Peace to supplement the ethic of the Just War. Yet to be effective, it must still answer several questions: What is the long-range goal of an ethic of a Just Peace? What can be done immediately toward this end? And, what, in sum, would be the chief dimensions of an ethic of a Just Peace?

The vision of an ethic of a Just Peace rests on the transformation of the prospects of necropolis into the prospects of cosmopolis. The institutions presently structured to preserve the peace actually bear with them systemic threats of destruction. They must be limited. This may involve, in the long run, abolishing war as a major social phenomenon and the dismantling of the institutional apparatus to conduct war. It is neither socially nor theologically inconceivable that major destructive forms of human relationships will have to be altered. Major institutions of the past have been changed. Manorial agriculture with its surfdom, chattel slavery with its dehumanization, and the divine right of rulers with its tyranny have all been done away with in centuries past. We must recover the theological insights that human institutions are "temporal" in nature and that they are therefore subject to alteration.

But a Just Peace ethic does not leap to that vision as an immediate prospect. As long as we live in history, in temporality, legitimate means of violence must be available to control evil and illegitimate violence. Thus, an ethic of a Just Peace continues to work closely with those moralists, social philosophers, and statesmen who attempt to define principles for the legitimate use of violence. But its chief focus is not that. It is instead the question of what understanding of social history, what shape of what institutions, and what values by which people interpreting the world are necessary or possible for the redefinition of human priorities. What will be more likely than present structures to lead to a world-wide human community of justice and equity and righteousness—a cosmopolis? Or, more modestly, how can we take the first steps toward the limitation of military-industrial complexes as entrenched social institutions so that the way is not left open for more idolatrous, less humanly sensitive institutions of violence to take command? The goal of an ethic of a Just Peace, then, is to develop values which, when incarnated in institutions, would provide both the sense of meaning or purpose and the organizational capacity to develop an urban-technological society that is at once free and ordered.

Several things can be done toward that end in the near future. Society must immediately commit itself to the development of counter-complexes. Theologically and ethically, we must identify and celebrate those centers of organizational vitality in the urban ethos that are already available to bear urban, cosmopolitan values. Preachers, secular or sacred, must spend their time and energy finding, understanding, interpreting, critically evaluating, and where appropriate, showing the legitimacy of such groups as the Blacks, the unions, the youth, and the humanistically concerned technological and scientific groups. The body of theological and social literature available for these purposes parallels the record of the historical development of the Military-Industrial Complex. It has been the minority report for more than a century and must now emerge into dominance.

Economically, voluntary support for such groups is absolutely necessary until they become sufficiently powerful to lay claim on the public purse and official institutionalization and until they develop a broad and democratic constituency that will support their aims. Theologically and practically, the tradition of tithing must be revived, whether the full portion is to be channeled through the churches or not. Sacrificial giving on the part of masses of people to the purposes of a Just Peace is all that will be able to compete economically with the economic austerity of millions of service personnel over the years of the development of the Complex. Churches and voluntary associations that have capital funds should review portfolios to see what kinds of ethical and social returns they get on their investments. Withdrawing funds from the corporations involved in the Military-Industrial Complex may have little effect on their operations directly, but investment in corporations dedicated, for example, to construction of a new urban environment or to international education and development may well have a highly constructive effect on the growth of alternative counter-complexes in the long run.

Politically, it is incumbent upon those concerned with a Just Peace to support representatives, senators, and bureaucrats who, from various motivations and perspectives, question military operations and policy. They keep the proper relation of the soldier and the state alive in the public mind and preserve, in at least modest degrees, civilian control over the military establishment. And today such questioning and demand for the rights of public scrutiny requires a political courage worthy of support. Politicians who have that courage also demand that the public receive full value for its tax dollar and that the governmental organization be efficiently run. Efficiency is not a moral category sufficient to itself, but it is an institutional virtue. In a complex as vast as that funded through the defense sector of the federal budget, there are numerous nooks and crannies where exploitation of the public purse, clumsy and inefficient operations in the name of public service, and personal boondoggles can take place. These must be controlled and supervised for the public good, even if seeking them out does not and cannot solve the fundamental problems of the Complex. It is possible that those politicians who ferret out such phenomena could provide the core political personnel for other and deeper investigations of national priority and for positive action on other complexes. Hence, one of the primary tasks of ethically concerned persons and organizations is simply to exercise their civic responsibility to support, by campaign contributions and mobilization of public sentiment, time, and vote, those political figures who are raising such questions.

Noticeable by its absence, perhaps, is the suggestion that demonstrations against the Pentagon or confrontation with the political parties, strategies taken during the last few years by groups interested in the transformation of the Military-Industrial Complex, can be truly effective. I do not want to ignore the critical roles these acts have played in raising public issues and in accomplishing a significant mass involvement in the questioning of national priorities. However, so far as I can see, these moments have generated no compelling redefinition of social values, no stable constituencies, few enduring institutions, and little coordinated programing. Thus, they are incapable of either weakening the power of the Military-Industrial Complex, withstanding a concerted attack from it, or solving the human problems of an urban industrial environment and Third World development, should, for example, the Viet Nam war somehow be ended. The present protests, then, must be judged as less pertinent to an ethic of a Just Peace than to the ethic of the Just War. That is, the peace demonstrators are protesting a policy and claiming that the war is unjust; they do not yet suggest an alternative polity. They are unhappy with the polity which makes present policy because of a principled critique of the present polity, not because of a socio-theological redefinition of good polity.

Beyond these actions in society at large, certain actions can be taken within the complex itself. The development of ethical guidelines for the Military-Industrial Complex should be revitalized. At the personal level of people's vocations, ethics of professional life must be developed. Few serious religious or secular moralists even among the chaplaincy have tried to come to grips with the morality of the military profession since Martin Luther's essay against the pacifists, "Can Soldiers Also Be Saved?" and the tracts written at the time of Cromwell's "New Model Army." The Nuremburg trials after World War II rendered direct judgment against persons caught up in a military-industrial complex of demonic proportions, but the full implications of those judgments have not been spelled out for the American situation. Although extensive manuals of discipline and codes of honor govern our armed forces, and although the professional soldier undergoes an elaborate socialization process through a pervasive etiquette that provides some moral guidance, little philosophical, social-psychological, theological, or ethical evaluation of these patterns occurs. The tendency of liberals, humanitarians, and socially concerned churchmen to avoid or oppose the military *a priori* must be overcome at least at this level. And, at even the pragmatic level, the military must take this dimension seriously. How soldiers comport themselves among the people is as important in military conflict as firepower, and more important in the battles for men's loyalties, political or ideological.

Further, the post-modern shape of warfare and of military-industrial institutions has brought about a new context and substance of vocational life for military, technological, and managerial personnel that has few, if any, traditional models and guides. What is proper behavior for those who serve in this context? What are the marks of responsible decision-making in the new, post-Protestant and post-individualistic structures of assembly-line, group thinking of post-urban institutions? What are the personal limits of vocational life and the proper boundaries of one's calling? Under what conditions is one morally required to get out, or break silence, or keep silence, or disobey orders? How are the institutional options for these choices kept open? These questions, beyond the boundary of this effort, are nevertheless crucial to a fuller view of ethics and the Military-Industrial Complex, and must be dealt with by the professional associations if professional standards of any kind are to survive. Otherwise, they will be dealt with by the feeble reed of conscience or by the self-interests of the corporations and the Department of Defense.

Also, at the personal level, we must recognize that since the Military-Industrial Complex remains in many respects relatively uncontrolled and unmitigated by counter-complexes, it tends to hurt people who are not definable as "the enemy." People get drawn into its vortex against their will or their judgment. Opponents are crushed by its overwhelming power. Most dramatically, draftees, selective conscientious objectors, and victims of war in other countries all feel the brunt of this complex and have few resources to protect themselves. Business and regions of the country are economically damaged by decisions to place contracts elsewhere. Those concerned about these problems must and, indeed, are organizing voluntary associations to engage in draft counseling, to lobby for legal exemption for selective conscientious objectors, to organize men in the service, to provide aid and relief to victims of war (especially when our nation is involved), and to find alternative business and industrial options.

More important, however, is the development of an ideological mind-set in the military and in defense-oriented corporations that relinquishes part of the responsibility for security—the larger part beyond purely military security. Social-political development agencies in other areas of government must be ready to assume increasing parts of the responsibility for defining the total national situation, including crises and threats, and for prescribing alternative approaches to them. To moderate the influence of the Military-Industrial Complex in this fashion is not going to be easy. Resistance to such proposals, however, could be lowered by modification of officers' training and increasing their exposure to non-military sciences. Just as important is the development of greater honesty about the ways capitalism and democracy actually function and the reasons that communism captures the loyalties of so many in underdeveloped portions of the world. The ideological polarization that resides in the Military-Industrial Complex is apparently more virulent than it needs to be. Finally, it is necessary to organize the voluntary associations and study groups in the services and in the corporations to investigate conversion to a peacetime economy. As the plans of the forties derive from the planning of the twenties and thirties, and as the structures of the seventies derive from the revised plans of the fifties and sixties, so the adjustment of the Military-Industrial Complex to the dilemmas of the next several decades must be worked out in present anticipation of major changes. Failure to do so will only bring the military under increased criticism and the corporations under pressure for ever-tighter controls. And if worse comes to worst, the situation may deteriorate into a series of non-governable, escalating domestic protests, or into international conflagration that destroys all prospects of urbane civilization. Necropolis will have won.

To avoid that, this volume proposes some steps toward the development of an ethic of a Just Peace, rooted in the Judeo-Christian mix of realism and vision, to supplement the ethic of a Just War. From a socio-political analysis of the problems of polity, we have come to a recognition of the need for the development of a set of theologically rooted values given body and force in institutions that enable us to move constructively toward a cosmopolitan commonwealth, and we have seen that specific moves can be made toward that end in society and in the Complex itself. What remains is the responsibility to summarize the main features of an ethic of a Just Peace. In contrast to the summary of the main ingredients and implications of the Just War doctrine, however, the accent here must fall on a list of accents, modes of interpretation, and moral priorities for social-political action under the overarching assumption that Just Peace demands a worthy ordering of power and an empowerment of social value.

1. *Institutions,* even political-military and economic institutions, *are theological and ethical in nature.* Large-scale organizations are formed around values, presuppositions, and goals that sustain them without continuous coercion. Manifestations like the Military-Industrial Complex are, thus, not merely the result of political preference and cannot be analyzed in terms of ordinary political ideology. Indeed, the quartet of primary ideological biases on the American scene—romanticism, localism, universalism, and reaction—is incapable of coming to grips with such anomalies. A social-religious perspective that attempts to preserve the realism and vision of the Judeo-Christian tradition is required.

2. *The Just Peace ethic requires construction of a decision machinery that allows the criteria of the Just War doctrine to become fully operative.* The utilization of Just War criteria to determine and judge policy is an important Judeo-Christian legacy, but it does not in itself provide the categories by which the empirical situation is to be discerned or structured. When the doctrine was developed there was no question about who was called upon to apply it. The prince was, and it was to the prince that the prophets and priests preached on the matter. But when large-scale information-gathering, -sorting and -transmitting agencies affect how the polity will perceive a situation, and when the authority of the polity is consolidated through complex representative electoral procedures and when the government embodying that authority must pass through layer upon layer of decision processes on matters of war and peace, the moral viability of judgments of whether the criteria of "last resort," "legitimate government," "just cause," etc., have been met depends upon the moral viability of those presuppositions, goals, and predispositions built into the deciding institutions. Therefore, an

ethic trying to work out and preserve the legacy of the Judeo-Christian tradition has to be developed that attempts to define the normative matrix of decision-making in social-political terms. And that ethic has to be conveyed not only to the princes, but to the people.

3. *Policy follows polity, and polity follows empowered piety.* That is, policy is the *ad hoc* product of the perceptions, dispositions, and assumptions of decisive social institutions. Decisive social institutions have deep roots, roots that penetrate social history and the values of the culture. And the institutions are given specific shape by the kinds and qualities of loyalties, values, and commitments that they represent and evoke. Any prescription for pervasive or sustained alterations of policy will of necessity be founded on a reformulation of values, a re-definition of loyalties and commitments, and the reconception and reordering of the structure of the polity. Thus, any serious strategy for change will work on a schedule proportionate to social and cultural rootedness of the decisive institutions. And it becomes necessary to deal explicitly with fundamental questions of what is in fact crucial for man's salvation and what is ultimately worthy of loyalty and commitment.

The negative side of this positive formulation that results will take time. Premature and unrealistic expectations on the basis of popular polls, or shifting sentiment, or short term activism can lead to disillusionment or cynicism that in turn can have negative consequences. They may lead to a radical decline in the viability of the social system because too few take responsibility for the continual task of carefully modifying it; they may lead to abandonment of the social system to those who would use it to forward the more destructive dimensions of social and cultural history; or they may lead to pseudo-revolution, the replacing of one set of leaders with another that does not fundamentally alter the structure of the overall society. Structural questions, rooted in ultimate concepts of worth and power, are decisive for an ethic of a Just Peace.

4. *The Judeo-Christian heritage demands continuing personal engagement in the reconstruction of the social system.* The tradition recognizes that because ultimately worthy power

never passes into the possession of a given society or set of institutions, social-political institutions are therefore temporal, fallible instruments, capable not only of salvation but of sin. But because they are temporal, they are also susceptible to human manipulation and pragmatic adjustment. At its best, then, the tradition demands humane institutions that, as matters of ultimate importance, both provide personal opportunities for meaning and require personal acknowledgment of responsibility for the commonwealth. Movement toward international social systems wherein the institutions of war can be abolished is therefore proper. But recognition of man's perennial temptation to exploit man demands the preservation of obedient and disciplined institutions capable of restraining violence and evil until a more universal commonwealth is attained.

5. *The urban environment,* for all its foibles and iniquities, *provides the best available social system for bearing the vision of cosmopolis.* In "post-city" urbanized culture, critical values of the Judeo-Christian heritage can be more readily actualized than they can in tribal, feudal, agrarian, or town settings, although clannish, aristocratic, familial, and bourgeois elements still lurk just below the surface of urban existence. The possibilities of new and broader definitions of peoplehood, continual new formations of covenanted groups, opportunities for taking upon oneself the sufferings of others in a quest for new qualities and shapes of life, developing a genuine pluralism, and transforming temporal structures through programmatic action toward the future are all resident in the urban and post-urban structures that point toward a cosmopolitan commonwealth. Thereby the possibilities of freedom from the bondages of past tyranny and natural necessity, and freedom to develop an order that is open becomes relatively more available to the human enterprise than in alternative existing patterns of life. For these possibilities to turn into realities, two things must be done. Social-political ideologies and institutions which threaten the viability of urban existence must be identified as leading to necropolis and challenged, for the possibilities of a Just Peace depend upon maintaining and extending both the values of and the social foundations for cosmopolitan life. And the dominant

American interpretation of the Judeo-Christian tradition, Protestantism, which on the one hand contributed so much to the development of the urban ethos and which on the other maintains so many of the valuational blocks to adequate coping with it, must undergo critical redefinition.

Beyond these five general propositions, a second set of priorities and motifs helps to show how the possibilities of a Just Peace may be more fully actualized.

6. *Security must be redefined.* Security cannot be attained by compulsive defensiveness nor can it be assured by proliferation of institutions and instruments of destruction that directly or indirectly threaten urban existence. Security in the Judeo-Christian tradition is properly seen in the capacity to trust that even the enemy is human, in the faith that human priorities are more significant than preservation of affluent life, and in the active hope that structures of reconciliation can be developed. Therefore, demythologizing the interpretation of enemies as dehumanized agents of demonic spirits is mandatory. The celebration of human gifts through institutions of human development is required, and the extension of human relationships and contacts must be risked. It is on these bases that genuine security can be developed; at the same time, it is realistically recognized that legitimatized but controlled institutions and instruments of coercion are required to prevent the corruption of these possibilities by violent exploitation.

7. *Countervailing complexes must be mobilized* against the inordinate power of a single dominant one to promote the possibility of a genuinely pluralistic definition of human needs and prescription of strategies. Only clusters of interlocking institutions dedicated to marginal humanity and urban development can effectively challenge the present order of the Military-Industrial Complex. Only comparable sets of institutions can redefine and adequately reinstitutionalize the critical values of the American civil religion. Only structurally similar organizations can provide alternative horizons for persons and for social-political constituencies. And only the patterned intricacy of a complex can develop the managerial-technological and contractual competence to address the massive social problems of

the nation and the world as we move into a post-urban environment.

8. *The ethic demands the democratization of economic as well as political power,* as well as the reverse in communist states. The capacity of a government to govern in an urban or post-urban society depends on the equitable provision of the necessities of life so that common participation in the quest for meaningful and quality existence can take place. People must be able to participate in the decisions that affect their destiny, whether economic or political, in order either to preserve and extend governmental legitimacy or to reduce direct coercion. Further, economic resources must be equitably distributed internationally. Pragmatically, it can be stated that only by developing relative parities between the affluent and the dispossessed nations can their jealousies and hostilities be reduced. And morally, it can be affirmed that an unrequited transfer of wealth to strengthen one's neighbor is a concrete implication of the Judeo-Christian concept of love. Only by developing strong international neighbors can our own or any nation's temptations to economic or cultural imperialism, an international form of egocentric sin, be mitigated, or our own or any nation's propensities for breaking a Just Peace or for misapplying the criteria of Just War out of ideological bias be compromised.

9. *We must redefine the personal meaning of and reconstruct the social possibilities of vocation.* Personal senses of purpose and wide-ranging opportunities for the exercise of competence are needed to sustain or develop any large-scale social system. Thus, opportunities must exist for professional commitment to the performance of meaningful tasks that link personal effort to service of the common good. And, in a larger sense, concepts of vocation that require and evolve a personal willingness to assume responsibility for the general shape of things through rich varieties of personal, fiscal, and group engagement are necessary to prevent the large, impersonal social systems of the present and future from being anti-personal. Not only must this take place for military and corporation personnel, but it must happen in fresh ways for the counter-complexes that must be developed. And this is particularly critical for those

Black, union, youth, and technological personnel for whom the possibilities of personal meaning linked to structures of socially significant opportunity are bleak.

10. *We must nurture by thought and action the fragile possibilities of a humane cosmopolis by realistically analyzing the prospects and resources for change and by moving specifically toward that end.* Such a proposition depends upon a vision that stretches human imagination and capacity, but that tries to take account of the limited horizons and opportunities of people.

If an ethic of Just Peace does become the center of national and international organization, the institutional and ideological foundations would be so laid that policy makers would be able more accurately to read a situation and more surely to attempt to discern when and how a Just War ethic could apply. In short, the Just War ethic can only function upon a sociological base organized around purposes of a Just Peace. Without this base, the principles to discriminate moral situations will become, as they have so recently in the United States' Southeast Asian policy, an occasion for self-justifying ideological pretension.

Failure to develop such a social-political ethic and make it operative will cause reliance on Just War theory alone. And it may be turned against the present structures and ideologies of the Military-Industrial Complex, and by extension against the government itself. For if a Just Peace is not established, increasing numbers will see no other resort than violence; increasing numbers will claim a just cause; increasing numbers will declare present authority illegitimate; with increasing numbers will come a greater hope of success in challenging the right of present institutions to remain, and a greater likelihood that more good will come out of overthrow than harm. In short, the failure of an ethic of a Just Peace will make more likely an ethic of Just War in the form of righteous revolution. Although some will feel more called to an ethic of tactical pacifism and non-violent non-cooperation whatever the consequences, we will have a government that cannot govern, a defense department that cannot defend, an industrial system that cannot produce, academic structures that can neither teach nor research, and an overall security that in all recognizable terms entails greater insecurity.

We are not, yet, at such a point. Redemptive social forces are available for mobilization and awareness of the need for change is growing. But unless we move toward a Just Peace, the Judeo-Christian tradition will have to mobilize intentionally toward revolution and non-cooperation. It would, should such extremities occur, have as its principal obligations to support the righteous revolutionaries while it demanded that they themselves be governed by the principles of Just War, and that the program of whatever ensues be governed by the vision, realism, and demands of the ethic of a Just Peace. And it would have the responsibility to protect the non-cooperators who would make society ungovernable. Thus within the present temporal order or beyond, the viability of modern, post-urban society depends in large measure on its approximation to a Just Peace.

—*Shalom*—

Notes

Chapter One

1. See David A. Martin, *Pacifism: An Historical and Sociological Study.*

2. Sir Herbert Read, *English Prose Style* (New York: Pantheon Books, 1952), p. 23, as quoted in Robert A. Nisbet, *Social Change and History*, p. 4. The entire section "History and Metaphor" is cogent and very helpful on this question.

3. Cf. my *Ethics and the Urban Ethos: An Essay in Social Analysis and Theological Reconstruction*, Chapter 5 (forthcoming).

4. The three major possibilities are most recently and most adequately treated, both historically and systematically, in Roland Bainton's *Christian Attitudes toward War and Peace*; Ralph Potter's *War and Moral Discourse* (cf. also Potter's "Christian Responses to Nuclear Warfare" [Unpublished Ph.D. dissertation, Harvard University, 1965], where categories are refined to five options); and Martin's *Pacifism*, especially part I.

5. See, for example, the essays in *God and the H-Bomb*, edited by Donald Keys. (New York: Bellmeadows Press, 1961). Also, cf. Robert Gardiner, "Nuclear Weapons: An Ethical Perspective" (Unpublished S.T.M. Thesis, 1969; Andover Newton Theological School).

6. Walter Rauschenbusch, *The Righteousness of the Kingdom*, ed. M. L. Stackhouse, p. 249.

7. See Reinhold Niebuhr's "Why the Christian Church Is Not Pacifist," in *Christianity and Power Politics*, pp. 1–32.

8. This, incidentally, is the problem that beset Martin Luther King, Jr. in his concept of militant non-violence, as can be seen in *The Trumpet of Conscience*, where he struggles against but finally does not quite break with the Pacifist tradition. In fact, in his reliance upon the enforcement of the law of the land by courts and upon protection for peaceful protest by police or National Guard, he depended upon structures of coercion and violence for which his theory does not account. And it is this failure that has partly discredited him with more realistic authors, although his significance remains highly pertinent to theological and ethical reflection in other regards.

9. See his *War and the Christian Conscience* and *The Just War*.

10. See the excellent contemporary discussion of this in Peter Berger and Richard Neuhaus, *Movement and Revolution*, especially part II.

11. These formulations are modifications of some of the major interpretations of Just War theory currently in debate. See Ralph Potter's invaluable Bibliographical Essay in *War and Moral Discourse* for an annotated guide to the basic literature. Also, cf. his *The Moral Logic of War,* Occasional Papers on Church and Conflict, No. 5 (United Presbyterian Church, 1969).

12. Perhaps the best catalogue of materials wherein these matters are debated, in regard to Viet Nam, often without conscious or explicit reference to Just War theory, is to be found in David Little's *American Foreign Policy and Moral Rhetoric.*

13. See, for example, debates over these matters in *Anti-Ballistic Missile: Yes or No?*, compiled by the Center for the Study of Democratic Institutions, with essays by Donald Brennan, Leon Johnson, Jerome Wiesner and George McGovern.

Chapter Two

1. See Jack Raymond, "The Growing Threat of Our Military-Industrial Complex," *Harvard Business Review* (May-June, 1968), p. 54.

2. Ibid., pp. 53 f.

3. Robert Bellah deals with the religious and moral character of presidential speeches in his outstanding article, "Civil Religion in America," in *The Religious Situation 1968,* ed. Donald Cutler, pp. 331–356.

4. This concern is the announced topic of Seymour Melman's forthcoming new work, *Pentagon Capitalism.* Cf. his "Business as Usual / National Suicide," *The Journal* (Dec. 1969), pp. 8–13.

5. The best book-length examples of recent Pacifist political analysis of these questions are John M. Swomley, *The Military Establishment,* and the earlier Fred J. Cook, *The Warfare State.* An excellent older example is Seymour Waldman, *Death and Profits.*

6. See Paul A. C. Koistinen, "The Hammer and the Sword: Labor, the Military, and Industrial Mobilization 1920–1945" (Ph.D. dissertation, U. of California, 1964). Also for a more recent example, see U.S. Senate, Committee on Government Operations, Report of the Permanent Subcommittee on Investigations, *Pyramiding Profits and Costs in the Missile Procurement Program* (G.P.O., 1968). Most recently, see Sen. William Proxmire, *Report from Wasteland.*

7. (Mental Health Research Institute, U. of Michigan, Photocopy reprint 144). Also published in *The Journal of Social Issues* (Vol. 21, No. 3, pp. 67–117) and reprinted in abridged form in Robert Perrucci and Marc Pilisuk, eds., *The Triple Revolution,* pp. 77–110, from which, since it is most accessible to the general reader, the subsequent references are taken. Note also the valuable bibliographic suggestions, especially in the first edition of the document.

8. See especially C. Wright Mills, *The Causes of World War III* **and** *The Power Elite,* and Irving L. Horowitz, ed., *The New Sociology.*

9. See, for example, Jack Raymond, *Power of the Pentagon* (New York: Harper, 1964). More recent supporting treatment can be found in Arnold Rose, *The Power Structure* and C. W. Borklund, *The Department of Defense.* The best brief treatment of the debate over Mills' thesis is *C. Wright Mills and The Power Elite,* Compiled by G. W. Domhoff and H. B. Ballard. The philosophical dimensions of this debate are brilliantly sorted out in Robert Paul Wolff, *The Poverty of Liberalism,* chapter 3.

10. Pilisuk and Hayden, op. cit. (see note 7 and text reference), p. 85.

11. Ibid., pp. 90 ff.

12. Ibid., pp. 92 ff.

13. Ibid., p. 99.

14. See John Kenneth Galbraith, *The New Industrial State* and *How to Control the Military.*

15. See especially, "The Corporations and the Complex," paper prepared for the Consultation on the Military-Industrial Complex sponsored by the Boston Industrial Mission, June, 1969, forthcoming in Norman Faramelli, ed., *Papers on the Military-Industrial Complex.*

16. Robert A. Gessert, "Whither the Military in U.S. Foreign Policy: Reflections on the Issue of the Military-Industrial Complex" (New York, Council on Religion and International Affairs, 1970).

17. Richard J. Barnet, *The Economy of Death,* p. 59.

18. Ibid., p. 98.

19. Ibid., p. 16.

20. Ibid., p. 64.

Chapter Three

1. Quincy Wright, *A Study of War.* I am also indebted in this section to the lectures on the subject by Professor Ritchie Lowry at Boston College, 1968. Cf. his article, "Two Arms: Changing Military Roles and the Military-Industrial Complex," *Social Problems,* Vol. 18, No. 1, Summer 1970, pp. 3–16.

2. Cf. Reinhold Niebuhr and Alan Heimert, *A Nation So Conceived.*

3. Morris Janowitz, *The Professional Soldier,* p. 151. Throughout this chapter, I am deeply indebted to Janowitz and to Samuel P. Huntington, *The Soldier and the State;* Paul Hammond, *Organizing for Defense;* and Alfred Vagts, *A History of Militarism.* These are valuable not only for their depth of insight and scholarship, but for their invaluable bibliographic resources.

4. Huntington, *The Soldier and the State.* There is no single volume that matches this one on the background of the military in richness of insight, bibliographic sources, and sustained interpretation—in spite of a rather pathetic last chapter.

5. Cf., especially, A. T. Mahan, *Armaments and Arbitration* and *Lessons of the War with Spain.*

6. Hammond, op. cit., p. 62.

7. Ibid., pp. 12–28.

8. Ibid. Hammond thinks the business model is more decisive than the German one (p. 23), but has to admit that it grew closer to the German model than Root intended (p. 26).

9. Janowitz, op. cit., p. 152.

10. Ibid.

11. Huntington, op. cit., p. 280.

12. Cf. Hammond, op. cit., pp. 87–92, from which this paragraph is largely drawn.

13. Ibid., pp. 94 f.

14. See Ray H. Abrams, *Preachers Present Arms.*

15. Cf. Huntington, op. cit., pp. 289–312.

16. The best presentation of these developments, with extensive bibliographical notes, is "The 'Industrial-Military Complex' in Historical Perspective: The Inter-War Years" by Paul A. C. Koistinen, in *The Journal of American History,* Vol. 56, no. 4, March 1970, pp. 819–39.

17. The best sources available on these developments are: A. A. Berle, *Economic Power and the Free Society;* Gardiner Means, *The Modern Corporation and Private Property;* F. X. Sutton et al., *The American Business Creed.*

18. See Arnold Rose, *The Power Structure,* and Robert Heilbroner, *The Making of Economic Society.*

19. See the excellent treatment of the scientific-political factors leading to this in Robert Batchelder's, *The Irreversible Decision.*

20. I use Galbraith's appropriate term. See chapter 2 above.

21. Robert Gardiner, in "Nuclear Weapons," chapter 2, has pointed out, however, that there is a minimum of face to face combat and that the humanity of the enemy is therefore avoided.

22. Samuel P. Huntington, "The Defense Establishment: Vested Interests and the Public Interest," p. 10.

23. This estimate and the breakdown of internal organization is taken from C. W. Borklund, *The Department of Defense,* to whom I am indebted for the clearest presentation available.

24. See the 1968 listing of corporations and amounts as published in *Aviation Week and Space Technology* (Dec. 2, 1968), pp. 80 ff.

25. F. Lundberg, *The Rich and Super Rich,* ed. E. Brand.

26. Many of these observations are derived from a series of consultations with members and former members of the Department of Defense or of corporations. One of the most fruitful was sponsored by the Boston Industrial Mission in Boston, December, 1968.

27. Borklund, op. cit., p. 92.

28. See James Ridgeway's fascinating exposé *The Closed Corporation.*

Chapter Four

1. *How to Control the Military*, p. 27.
2. The debates concerning the role of Calvinistic Protestantism in the development of modern industrial, urban society have continued for more than a century and focus on the writing of and about Max Weber. See S. M. Eisenstadt, ed., *The Protestant Ethic and Modernization;* A. T. Van Leeuwen, *Christianity in World History,* especially chapter 6; Samuel Huntington, *The Soldier and the State,* especially pp. 20 ff; and Michael Walzer, *The Revolution of the Saints.*
3. Cf. Victor C. Ferkiss, *Technological Man.*
4. *The Professional Soldier,* pp. 86–7.
5. Cf. Hans Speier, *Social Order and the Risks of War,* especially pp. 8–15.
6. Robert S. McNamara, *The Essence of Security,* p. 58. He suggests, among other things, that the defensive planning of the Military-Industrial Complex is not as attributable to authoritarian personality or crypto-fascism, as many contemporary critics of the military are inclined to claim, as it is to a specific combination of cultural values and social responsibilities.
7. Emile Durkheim, *The Division of Labor in Society,* is still the classic statement of these motifs.
8. Melvin Laird, *A House Divided,* p. 16.
9. See especially Janowitz, *The Professional Soldier.*
10. Cf. Charles J. Hitch and Roland N. McKean, *The Economics of Defense in the Nuclear Age.*
11. "The Problem of Momentum," in *A. B. M.,* ed. by Abram Chayes and Jerome Wiesner, pp. 145 f.
12. See especially Janowitz, op. cit., part V and Huntington, op. cit., chapter 3, for pertinent discussions of the military "mind" and "ideology."
13. See, for example, Thomas C. Schelling, *Arms and Influence.*
14. Cf. Hitch & McKean, op. cit., and McNamara, op. cit.
15. A small sect with another set of interpretations can be found clustered around the Arms Control and Disarmament Agency. But they are only marginally influential. Cf., especially Roger E. Bolton, ed., *Defense and Disarmament,* and Robert Gard, Jr., "Arms Control and National Security" in A. A. Jordan, ed. *Issues of National Security in the 1970's.*
16. *A House Divided.*
17. Ibid., p. 4.
18. Ibid., p. 11.
19. Ibid., p. 13.
20. Ibid., p. 13.
21. Ibid., p. 19. Laird also praises John Foster Dulles for having

a grasp of these truths (pp. 25 f.). It is notable that Dulles was an important figure in Protestant lay organizations as well as in the defense establishment.

22. Ibid., p. 32.
23. Ibid., p. 49.
24. Ibid., p. 79.
25. Ibid., p. 90.
26. *The Essence of Security,* p. viii.
27. Ibid., p. viii.
28. Ibid., p. 4.
29. Ibid., p. 5.
30. Ibid., p. 8.
31. Ibid., p. 13.
32. Ibid., p. 51.
33. Ibid., p. 53.
34. Ibid., p. 56.
35. Ibid., p. 59.
36. Ibid., p. 61.
37. Ibid., p. 109.
38. Ibid., p. 119.
39. Ibid., p. 149.

Selected bibliography

Abrams, Ray H. *Preachers Present Arms*. Scottdale, Pa.: Herald Press, 1969.

Advisory Committee on Government Programs in the Behavioral Sciences, National Research Council. *The Behavioral Sciences and the Federal Government*. Washington: National Academy of Sciences, 1968.

Andrezjewski, Stanislaw. *Military Organization and Society*. New York: Routledge, 1954.

Austin, Alan D., ed. *The Revolutionary Imperative*. Nashville, Tenn.: Board of Education of the Methodist Church, 1966.

Bainton, Roland H. *Christian Attitudes toward War and Peace*. Nashville, Tenn.: Abingdon Press, 1960.

Barnet, Richard J. *The Economy of Death*. New York: Atheneum, 1970.

———. *Intervention and Revolution*. New York: World Publishing Co., 1968.

Batchelder, Robert C. *The Irreversible Decision*. Boston: Houghton Mifflin Co., 1961.

Baumgartner, John Stanley. *The Lonely Warriors: A Case for the Military Industrial Complex*. Los Angeles: Nash Publishing, 1970.

Bellah, Robert. "Civil Religion in America," in *The Religious Situation, 1968*. ed. by Donald Cutler. Boston: Beacon Press, 1968.

Berger, Peter and Neuhaus, Richard. *Movement and Revolution*. Garden City, N.J.: Doubleday, 1970.

Berle, A. A. *Economic Power and The Free Society*. New York: Harper, 1958.

Bolton, Roger E., ed. *Defense and Disarmament.* Englewood Cliffs, N.J.: Prentice-Hall, 1966.

Borklund, C. W. *The Department of Defense.* New York: Frederick A. Praeger, 1968.

Bramson, Leon, et al., eds. *War: Studies from Psychology, Sociology, Anthropology.* New York: Basic Books, 1964.

Center for the Study of Democratic Institutions. *Anti-Ballistic Missile: Yes or No?* New York: Hill & Wang, 1968.

Chayes, Abram and Wiesner, Jerome, eds. *ABM.* New York: Harper & Row, 1969.

Clark, Harold F. and Sloan, Harold S. *Classrooms in the Military: An Account of Education in the Armed Forces of the United States.* New York: Bureau of Publications, Columbia University, 1966.

Coffin, Tristram. *The Armed Society.* Baltimore: Penguin Books, 1964.

Cook, Fred. *The Warfare State.* New York: The Macmillan Co., 1962.

Coser, Lewis. *The Functions of Social Conflict.* New York: The Free Press, 1956.

Daedalus. *Perspectives on Business.* Vol. 98, No. 1 (Winter, 1969).

Deitchman, Seymour J. *Limited War and American Defense Policy.* Revised ed. Cambridge, Mass.: The M.I.T. Press, 1969.

Domhoff, G. William and Ballard, Hoyt B. *C. Wright Mills and the Power Elite.* Boston: Beacon Press, 1968.

Drinan, Fr. Robert. *Vietnam and Armageddon.* New York: Sheed and Ward, 1970.

Drucker, Peter F. *The Age of Discontinuity.* New York: Harper & Row, 1969.

Durkheim, Emile. *The Division of Labor in Society.* New York: Macmillan, 1933.

Eisenstadt, S. M., ed. *The Protestant Ethic and Modernization.* New York: Basic Books, 1968.

Evans, Donald, ed. *Peace, Power, Protest.* Toronto: Ryerson Press, 1967.

Faramelli, Norman. *Papers on the Military-Industrial Complex*, forthcoming.

Ferkiss, Victor C. *Technological Man*. New York: George Braziller, 1969.

Galbraith, John K. *How To Control the Military*. New York: New American Library, Inc., 1969.

———. *The New Industrial State*. Boston: Houghton Mifflin Co., 1967.

Gardiner, Robert. "Nuclear Weapons: An Ethical Perspective." S.T.M. dissertation, Andover Newton Theological School, 1969.

Gessert, Robert. "Whither the Military in U.S. Foreign Policy: Reflections on the Issue of the Military Industrial Complex." New York: Council on Religion and International Affairs, 1970.

Halpern, Manfred. *The Morality and Politics of Intervention*. New York: The Council on Religion and International Affairs, 1969.

Hamilton, Michael P., ed. *The Viet Nam War: Christian Perspectives*. Grand Rapids, Mich.: William B. Eerdmans Publishing Co., 1967.

Hammond, Paul. *Organizing For Defense*. Princeton, N.J.: Princeton University Press, 1961.

Heilbroner, Robert L. *The Great Ascent*. New York: Harper & Row, 1963.

———. *The Making of Economic Society*. Englewood Cliffs, N.J.: Prentice-Hall, 1962.

Hitch, Charles J. and McKean, Roland N. *The Economics of Defense in the Nuclear Age*. New York: Atheneum, 1966.

Hodgson, Peter E. *Nuclear Physics in Peace and War*. New York: Hawthorn Books, 1961.

Horowitz, Irving Louis, ed. *The New Sociology*. New York: Oxford University Press, 1964.

———. ed. *The Rise and Fall of Project Camelot*. Cambridge Mass.: The M.I.T. Press, 1967.

Huntington, Samuel P. *The Soldier and the State*. Cambridge, Mass.: Harvard University Press, Belknap Press, 1967.

————. "The Defense Establishment: Vested Interests and the Public Interest," *The Military-Industrial Complex and U.S. Foreign Policy*, edited by Omer L. Carey. Pullman, Washington: Washington State University Press, 1969.

Janowitz, Morris. *The New Military*. New York: Russell Sage Foundation, 1964.

————. *The Professional Soldier*. New York: The Free Press, 1960.

————. *Sociology and the Military Establishment*. New York: Russell Sage Foundation, 1965.

Jordan, Amos A. *Issues of National Security in the 1970's*. New York: Frederick A. Praeger, 1967.

King, Martin Luther. *The Trumpet of Conscience*. New York: Harper & Row, 1968.

Kissinger, Henry A. *Nuclear Weapons and Foreign Policy*. Garden City, N.Y.: Doubleday & Co., 1958.

Koistinen, Paul. A. C. "The Hammer and the Sword." Unpublished Ph.D. dissertation, University of California, 1964.

————. "The 'Industrial-Military Complex' in Historical Perspective: The Inter-War Years," *The Journal of American History*. Vol. 56, March, 1970.

Kolko, Gabriel. *The Roots of American Foreign Policy*. Boston: Beacon Press, 1969.

Laird, Melvin R. *A House Divided: America's Strategy Gap*. Chicago: Henry Regnery Co., 1962.

Lapp, Ralph E. *The Weapons Culture*. New York: W. W. Norton & Co., 1968.

Lens, Sidney. *The Military-Industrial Complex*. Philadelphia: Pilgrim Press, 1970.

Little, David. *American Foreign Policy and Moral Rhetoric: The Example of Viet Nam*. New York: The Council on Religion and International Affairs, 1969.

Lowry, Ritchie, P. "Changing Military Roles." *Rural Sociology*, Vol. 30 (June, 1965), pp. 219–225.

————. "Two Arms: Changing Military Roles and the Military-Industrial Complex," *Social Problems*, Vol. 18, No. 1, (Summer, 1970), pp. 3–16.

Lundberg, F. *The Rich and the Super Rich*. Edited by E. Brand. New York: Lyle Stuart, 1969.

McFarland, Andrew S. *Power and Leadership in Pluralist Systems*. Stanford, Calif.: Stanford University Press, 1969.

McNamara, Robert S. *The Essence of Security*. New York: Harper & Row, 1968.

Mahan, A. T. *Armaments and Arbitration*. New York: Harper Brothers, 1912.

————. *Lessons of the War with Spain*. Boston: Little, Brown and Company, 1899.

Mansfield, Edwin, ed. *Defense, Science, and Public Policy*. New York: W. W. Norton & Co., 1968.

Marcus, Sumner. "Studies of Defense Contracting." *Harvard Business Review*. Vol. 42. (May-June, 1964), pp. 20 ff.

Martin, David A. *Pacifism: An Historical and Sociological Study*. New York: Schocken Books, 1965.

Means, Gardiner. *The Modern Corporation and Private Property*. New York: Macmillan, 1932.

Melman, Seymour. "Business as Usual/National Suicide," *The Journal* (Dec., 1969), pp. 8–13.

————. *Our Depleted Society*. New York: Holt, Rinehart and Winston, 1965.

————. *The Political Economy of War*. New York: McGraw-Hill, 1970.

Miller, Arthur S. "The Rise of the Techno-Corporate State in America." *Bulletin of the Atomic Scientist: Science and Public Affairs*. Vol. 25.

Millis, Walter. *Arms and Men: A Study of American Military History*. New York: G. P. Putnam's Sons, 1958.

Mills, C. Wright. *The Causes of World War III*. New York: Simon and Schuster, 1958.

————. *The Power Elite*. New York: Oxford University Press, 1959.

Mollenhoff, Clark R., *The Pentagon*. New York: G. P. Putnam's Sons, 1967.

National Council of the Churches of Christ in the U.S.A. *Imperatives of Peace and Responsibilities of Power*. New

York: Department of International Affairs, National Council of Churches, 1968.

Niebuhr, Reinhold, *Christianity and Power Politics*. New York: Charles Scribner's Sons, 1940.

————. *Christian Realism and Political Problems*. New York: Charles Scribner's Sons, 1953.

————. *Faith and Politics*. Edited by Ronald H. Stone. New York: George Braziller, 1968.

Niebuhr, Reinhold and Heimert, Alan. *A Nation So Conceived*. New York: Charles Scribner's Sons, 1963.

Nieburg, H. L. *In the Name of Science*. Chicago: Quadrangle Books, 1966.

Nisbet, Robert A. *Social Change and History*. New York: Oxford University Press, 1969.

Obenhaus, Victor. *Ethics for an Industrial Age: A Christian Inquiry*. New York: Harper & Row, 1965.

Oglesby, Carl, and Shaull, Richard. *Containment and Change*. New York: The Macmillan Co., 1967.

Perlo, Victor. *Militarism and Industry*. New York: International Publishers, 1963.

Perrucci, Robert and Pilisuk, Marc. *The Triple Revolution*. Boston: Little, Brown and Company, 1968.

Pilisuk, Marc and Hayden, Thomas. *Is There a Military Industrial Complex Which Prevents Peace? Consensus and Countervailing Power in Pluralistic Systems*. Mental Health Research Institute, University of Michigan, 1964.

Potter, Ralph B. *The Moral Logic of War*. Occasional Papers on the Church and Conflict, No. 5. Philadelphia: United Presbyterian Church U.S.A., 1969.

————. *War and Moral Discourse*. Richmond, Virginia: John Knox Press, 1969.

Proxmire, William. *Report from Wasteland*. New York: Praeger Publishers, 1970.

Ramsey, Paul. *The Just War*. New York: Charles Scribner's Sons, 1968.

————. *War and the Christian Conscience*. Durham, N.C.: Duke University Press, 1961.

Rauschenbusch, Walter. *The Righteousness of the Kingdom.* Edited by Max L. Stackhouse, Nashville, Tenn.: Abingdon Press, 1968.

Raymond, Jack. "The Growing Threat of Our Military-Industrial Complex," *Harvard Business Review.* Vol. 46 (May–June, 1968), pp. 53–64.

Ridgeway, James. *The Closed Corporation.* New York: Random House, 1968.

Rikon, Irving. *Peace As It Can Be.* New York: Philosophical Library, 1970.

Rose, Arnold M. *The Power Structure.* New York: Oxford University Press, 1967.

Rutenber, Culbert. *The Dagger and the Cross.* Nyack, N.Y.: Fellowship Publications, 1958.

Schelling, Thomas C. *Arms and Influence.* New Haven, Conn.: Yale University Press, 1966.

Schwarz, Urs. *American Strategy: A New Perspective.* Garden City, N.Y.: Doubleday & Co., 1966.

Speier, Hans. *Social Order and the Risks of War.* Cambridge, Mass.: The M.I.T. Press, 1952.

Stackhouse, Max L. *Ethics and the Urban Ethos: An Essay in Social Analysis and Theological Reconstruction.* Forthcoming.

Steinkraus, Warren E. "War and the Philosopher's Duty." In *The Critique of War,* edited by Robert Ginsberg. Chicago: Henry Regnery Co., 1969.

Sutton, F. X., et al. *The American Business Creed.* New York: Schocken Books, 1962.

Swomley, John M. *The Military Establishment.* Boston: Beacon Press, 1964.

Tucker, Robert W. *The Just War.* Baltimore: Johns Hopkins Press, 1960.

Vagts, Alfred. *A History of Militarism, Civilian and Military.* Revised ed. New York: The Free Press, 1959.

Van Leewuen, A. T. *Christianity in World History.* New York: Charles Scribner's Sons, 1964. Especially chapter 6.

Waldman, Seymour. *Death and Profits.* New York: Macmillan, 1932.

Walzer, Michael. *The Revolution of the Saints*. Cambridge, Mass.: Harvard University Press, 1968.

Weidenbaum, Murray. *The Modern Public Sector*. New York: Basic Books, 1969.

Weisner, Jerome B. *Where Science and Politics Meet*. New York: McGraw-Hill, 1965.

Wells, Donald A. *The War Myth*. New York: Pegasus, 1968.

Wolff, Robert Paul. *The Poverty of Liberalism*. Boston: Beacon Press, 1968.

Wright, Quincy. *A Study of War*. Chicago: University of Chicago Press, 1942 and 1964.

301.59
St 775